FÉNEL[

Talking with God

FÉNELON

Talking with God

by François Fénelon

Modern English Version by
Hal M. Helms

PARACLETE PRESS
Brewster, Massachusetts

Library of Congress Cataloging-in-Publication Data

Fénelon, François de Salignac de La Mothe–, 1651-1715.
  [Lettres spirituelles. English]
  Fénelon: talking with God / by François Fénelon; modern English version by Hal M. Helms.
     p.cm.
  ISBN: 1-55725-180-0 (pbk.: alk. paper)
  1. Meditations. 2. Spiritual life—Catholic Church.
3. Catholic Church—Doctrines. I. Helms, Hal McElwaine.
II. Title.
BX2183.F33213 1997
248.4'82–dc21   97-5619
                                                 CIP

10 9 8 7 6 5 4

Published by Paraclete Press
Brewster, Massachusetts
www.paracletepress.com
Printed in the United States of America

Cover artwork credit: Rijksmuseum Amsterdam

Table of Contents

Talking with God

Introduction

How does one "hear" God? The Bible speaks over and over again about listening and hearing his voice. The psalmist said, "Our God comes, he does not keep silence. . . . Hear, O my people, and I will speak." (Psalm 50) Yet for the most part, do we expect to hear him speak to us?

Fénelon has been a trusted counselor for myriads of Christians for more than two centuries. He came strongly to believe that God is a living, active presence and voice in the Christian's life. He did not hesitate to give the wisest word he knew to those who asked his advice. He was frank in sharing his own difficulties and struggles as life dealt him unexpected and difficult blows. But out of that crucible of suffering and misunderstanding, he listened for God's word, God's will, God's message to him.

More often than not, God is speaking to us in the so-called circumstances of life. If we look at them on a merely human plane, we may become confused, discouraged and totally disillusioned with life. Self-pity and accusation of others may be our daily bread. If we look at them as being part of God's loving dealing with us, weaning us away from the false, binding us more firmly to that which is eternal, we begin to "hear" God's word coming through these conditions.

This compilation of Fénelon's letters and words of counsel can encourage us as it has generations before us, to *listen* and *hear* the voice of the Good Shepherd.

one

How to Talk with God

Talk with God with the thoughts of which your heart is full. If you enjoy the presence of God, if you feel drawn to love him, tell him so. Such sensible fervor will make the time of prayer fly without exhausting you, for all you will have to do is to pour forth from your abundance and say what you feel.

But what, you ask, are you to do in times of dryness, inner resistance, and coldness? Do just the same thing. Say equally what is in your heart. Tell God that you no longer feel any love for him, that all is a terrible blank to you, that he wearies you, that his presence does not even move you, that you long to leave him for the most trifling occupation, and that you will not feel happy till you have left him and can turn to thinking about yourself. Tell him all the evil you know about yourself.

So how can we even ask what there is to talk to God about? Alas, there is only too much! But when you tell him about your miseries, ask him to cure them. Say to him, "O my God, behold my ingratitude, my inconstancy, my infidelity. Take my heart, for I do not know how to give it to you. Give me an inner distaste for external things; give me crosses necessary to bring me back under your yoke. Have mercy on me in spite of myself!" In this way either God's mercies or your own miseries will always give you enough to talk to him about. The subject will never be exhausted!

In either of these two states I have described, tell him without hesitation everything that comes into your head, with the simplicity and familiarity of a little child sitting on its mother's knee.

two

Desiring God's Will

Love desires that God would give us what we need and that he would have less regard to our frailty than to the purity of our intentions. Love even covers our trifling defects and purifies us like a consuming fire. "The Spirit intercedes for the saints in accordance with God's will," for "We do not know how we ought to pray,"[1] and in our ignorance, we frequently ask what would be injurious. We would, for instance, like to have fervor of devotion, distinct emotions of joy, and perfections which others could see. But these would serve to nourish the life of self within us and develop a confidence in our own strength. Love, however, leads us on and abandons us, as it were, to the operations of grace, putting us entirely at the disposal of God's will. Thus it prepares us for all his secret designs.

Then we will have all things and yet nothing. What God gives is precisely what we should have desired to ask. For we will have whatever he wills, and only that. Thus, this state contains all prayer: it is a work of the heart which includes all its desire. The Spirit prays within us for those very things which the Spirit himself wills to give us. Even when we are occupied with outward things, when our thoughts are drawn off by what our duties or position may require, we still carry within us a constantly burning fire which is not, and cannot be put out. It nourishes a secret prayer and is like a lamp continually lighted before the throne of God. "I slept, but my heart was awake."[2] "Blessed are those servants whom the Lord when he comes, shall find watching."[3]

[1] Romans 8:27, 26 (NIV).
[2] Song of Solomon 5:2 (NRSV).
[3] St. Luke 12:37 (KJV, SLIGHTLY MODIFIED).

three

On True Prayer of the Heart

True prayer is simply another name for the love of God. Its excellence does not consist in the multitude of our words, for our Father knows what we need before we ask him.[1] True prayer is that of the heart, and the heart prays only for what it desires. *To pray*, then, is *to desire or long for,* but to desire what God would have us desire. He who asks, but not from the bottom of his heart, is mistaken in thinking that he prays. Even though he spends days in reciting prayers in meditation, or in forcing himself in religious exercises, he does not once truly pray if he really does not *desire and yearn for* the things he pretends to ask.

Oh, how few there are who pray! How few are they who desire what is truly good! Crosses, external and internal humiliation, the renunciation of our own wills, the death of self, and the establishment of God's throne upon the ruins of self-love—these are indeed good. If we do not desire these, we do not truly pray. To desire them seriously, soberly, constantly, and with reference to all the details of life, this is true prayer. Not to desire them, and yet to suppose we pray is an illusion like that of the wretched souls who delude themselves that they are happy. Alas! how many souls, full of self and of an imaginary desire for perfection in the midst of hosts of willful disobediences, have never yet uttered this true prayer of the heart. It is in reference to this that St. Augustine says, *He who loves little, prays little; he who loves much, prays much.*

On the other hand, the heart in which the true love of God and true desire exist never ceases to pray. Love, hidden in the bottom of the soul, prays without ceasing, even when the mind is drawn another way. God continually beholds the desire which he has himself implanted in the soul. Though we may at times be unconscious of its existence, the heart is touched by it. Such a hidden desire in the soul ceaselessly draws God's mercies. It is that Spirit which, according to St. Paul, helps us in our weakness and intercedes for us "with sighs too deep for words."[2]

[1] St. Matthew 6:8.
[2] Romans 8:26 (NRSV).

four

On Maintaining a Life of Prayer

Two main points of attention are necessary to maintain a constant spirit of prayer that unites us with God. We must continually seek to cherish it, and we must avoid everything that tends to make us lose it.

In order to cherish it, we should follow a regular course of reading; we must have appointed times of secret prayer and frequently recall our minds consciously to God during the day. We should make use of quiet days or retreats when we feel the need of them or when they are advised by those more experienced than we whose counsel we seek, and when our other responsibilities allow for them.

We should be very afraid of all things that have a tendency to make us lose this state of prayer and be very careful to avoid them. Thus we should avoid those worldly activities and associates which turn our minds in the wrong direction, and those pleasures which excite the passions. We should avoid everything calculated to awaken the love of the world and those old inclinations that have caused us so much trouble.

There are many details that might apply in dealing with cherishing the spirit of prayer and avoiding that which works against it. Because each individual case has features peculiar to itself, only general directions can be given here.

We should choose books which instruct us in our duty and in our faults; which, while they point to the greatness of God, teach us what our duty is to him and how very far we are from perfecting it. We should not seek those emotional publications which melt and sentimentalize the heart. The tree must bear fruit. We can only judge the life of the root by the fruit it bears.[1]

The first effect of a sincere love is an earnest desire to know all that we ought to do to gratify the one we love. Any other desire is an indication that we love ourselves under a pretense of loving God. It shows that we are seeking an empty and deceitful consolation in him, that we want to use God for our pleasure, instead of sacrificing that pleasure for his glory. God forbid that his children should love him so! Cost what it may, if we want truly to love him, we must know what he requires of us and try to do it without reservation.

Periods of secret prayer must be determined by the time available, the disposition, the condition, and the inward leading of each individual.

A necessary foundation to prayer is meditating and thinking on the great truths which God has revealed. We should be familiar with all the mysteries of Jesus Christ and the truths of his gospel. Our souls should be colored by them and penetrated by them as wool is by dye. These truths should become so familiar to us that we acquire the habit of forming no judgment except in their light, that they may be our only guide in what we do, as the rays of the sun are our only light in what we see.

It is when these truths are inwardly incorporated in us that our praying begins to be real and fruitful. Up to that point prayer was but a shadow. We thought we had penetrated to the inmost depths of the gospel, when in truth we had barely set foot upon its border. All our most tender and ardent feelings, our firmest resolutions, our clearest and most distant visions were, in reality, but the rough and shapeless mass from which God would hew his likeness in us.

When his celestial rays begin to shine within us, then we see in the true light. Then we instantaneously assent to every truth in the same way we admit, without any process of reasoning, the splendor of the sun the moment we behold its rising beams. Our union with God must be the result of our faithfulness in doing and enduring all that he wills for us.

Our meditations should become deeper and more inward every day. I say *deeper*, because by frequent and humble meditation upon God's truth, we penetrate further and further in search of new treasures; and *more inward,* because as we seek more and more to enter into these truths, they penetrate into the very substance of our souls. Then it will be that a simple word will go further than a whole sermon.

Our meditation should not be subtle or composed of long reasonings. Simple and natural reflections from the subject of our thoughts is all that is required. We need take but a few truths, meditate upon these without hurry, without effort, and without seeking for far-fetched reflections. Every truth should be considered with reference to its practical bearing in our lives. To receive it without using all means to put it faithfully into practice at at whatever cost is to "hold the truth in unrighteousness."[2] It is a resistance to the truth that has been impressed upon us and, of course, is resistance to the Holy Spirit. This is the most terrible of all unfaithfulness.

As to a method of praying, each one must be guided by his or her own experience. If some find themselves aided in using a strict method, they need not depart from it. Those who cannot so confine themselves may make use of their own mode without judging that which has proved helpful to so many others. A method is intended to assist.

Growth in prayer is indicated by a growth in simplicity and steadiness in our attitude. Our conversation with God resembles that with a friend. At first there are a thousand things to be told, and just as many to be asked. After a time, however, these diminish, while the pleasure of being together does not. Everything has been said, but the satisfaction of seeing each other, of feeling that one is near the other, can be felt without conversation. The silence is eloquent and mutually understood. Each feels that the other is in perfect harmony with him, and that their two hearts are continuously being poured into each other, becoming one.

It is the same way in prayer. Our communion with God becomes a simple and familiar union, far beyond the need of words. But let it be remembered that God must initiate this kind of prayer within us. Nothing would be more rash nor more dangerous than to dare to attempt it of ourselves. We must allow ourselves to be led step by step, by someone conversant with the ways of God and who may lay the immovable foundations of correct teaching and of the complete death of self in everything.

Our practice of prayer in seclusion or private retirement must be regulated by our leisure and our other needs. We must attend to duty before we seek enjoyment in spiritual exercises. The man who has public duties and spends the time meditating that he should be giving to his duties, would miss God while he sought to be united to him. The true union with God is to do his will without ceasing in every duty of life, in spite of all natural disinclination, and however disagreeable or mortifying it may be to our self will.

We must, however, reserve the necessary time that we may seek God alone in prayer. Those who have positions of importance to fill usually have so many indispensable duties to perform, that without the greatest care in the management of their time, there will be none left to be alone with God. If they have ever so little inclination for foolish amusement, the hours that belong to God and their neighbor disappear altogether.

We must be firm in observing our rules. This strictness seems excessive, but without it everything falls into confusion. We will become dissipated, relaxed, and spiritually weak. We will be unconsciously drawn away from God, surrendering ourselves to all our pleasures, and only begin to see that we have wandered when it is almost hopeless to think of trying to return.

Prayer, prayer! this is our only safety. "Praise be to God who has not rejected my prayer, or withheld his love from me."[3] To be faithful in prayer it is indispensable that we arrange all the activities of the day with a regularity that nothing can disturb.

[1] Cf. St. Matthew 7:15–20.
[2] Romans 1:18 (KJV).
[3] Psalm 66:20 (NIV).

five

Choosing Companions Wisely

"He who walks with the wise grows wise, but a companion of fools suffers harm."[1]

Would you truly know a man? Observe who are his companions! How can he who loves God and who loves nothing except in and for God, enjoy the intimate companionship of those who neither love nor know God, and who look upon love of him as a weakness? Can a heart full of God and deeply aware of its own frailty, ever rest and be at ease with those who do not have feelings in common with it—who, indeed, are ever seeking to rob it of its treasure? Their delights are incompatible with the pleasures which faith brings.

I am well aware that we cannot, indeed, *ought not* to break with those friends to whom we are bound by our appreciation of their natural amiability, by their assistance, by ties of sincere friendship, or by the regard growing out of mutual helpfulness. Friends whom we have treated with a certain familiarity and confidence would be wounded to the quick if we were to separate from them entirely. We must gently and imperceptibly diminish our association with them without declaring abruptly our alteration of feeling. We may see them in private and relate to them more closely than to less intimate friends. We may confide to them those matters in which their integrity and friendship enable them to give us good advice and share our thoughts. In short, we may continue to serve them and show them a cordial friendship without allowing our hearts to be impeded or confused by them.

Without this precaution, our state is perilous indeed! If we do not from the first boldly make our commitment to the Lord entirely free and independent from our unregenerate friends, that commitment is threatened with a speedy downfall. If we are of a yielding disposition and passionate nature, it is certain that such friends, even the best-intentioned ones, will lead us astray. They may be good, honest, faithful, and they may have all those qualities which make friendship perfect in the eye of the world, but for us they are infected, and their good-naturedness only makes them more dangerous. Those friendships that do not have this estimable character should be sacrificed at once. Blessed are we when a sacrifice that ought to cost us so little may avail to give us so precious a security for our eternal salvation!

[1] Proverbs 13:20 (NIV).

The Practice of Humility

Always fear haughtiness. Fear overconfidence in your own ideas, and determination in your way of speaking. Be meek and humble of heart—that is to say, your meekness should come from a sincere humility. Bitterness and lack of moderation come only from pride.

If you wish to become meek, you must humble yourself. Make yourself little in the depths of your heart. A humble heart is always gentle and capable of being easily led in its center, even if on the surface it may seem rough through unexpected outbursts of a sharp and irritable temper. Watch, pray, and work at this. Bear with yourself without flattering yourself. Let your spiritual reading and your prayer help you to know yourself better, to correct yourself, and to overcome your natural temperament in the presence of God.

seven

Conforming to the Life of Jesus

We are called to imitate Jesus: live as he lived, think as he thought, and be conformed to his image. This is the mark of our sanctification.

What a contrast! Nothingness strives to be something, and the Omnipotent becomes nothing! I will be nothing with you, Lord! I offer you the pride and vanity which have possessed me. Help my will in this resolve! Protect me from occasions of stumbling. Turn away my eyes from beholding vanity.[1] Let me behold nothing but you, and myself in your presence, that I may understand what I am and what you are.

Jesus Christ was born in a stable. He had to flee into Egypt; thirty years of his life were spent in a workshop. He suffered hunger, thirst, and weariness. He was poor,

17

despised, and miserable. He taught the truths of heaven, and no one would listen to him. The great and the wise persecuted and took him, subjected him to frightful torments, treated him as a slave, and put him to death between two criminals. They chose to give liberty to a robber rather than allow him to escape. Such was the life which our Lord chose. We, on the other hand, are horrified at any kind of humiliation and cannot bear the slightest appearance of contempt.

Let us compare our lives with that of Jesus, remembering that he was the Master and we are the servants; that he was all-powerful and that we are but weakness; that he was abased and that we are exalted. Let us so constantly bear our wretchedness in mind that we may have nothing but contempt for ourselves. With what face can we despise others and dwell upon their faults, when we ourselves are filled with nothing else? Let us begin to walk in the path which our Savior has marked out, for it is the only one that can lead us to him.

How can we expect to find Jesus if we do not seek him in the states of his earthly life, in loneliness and silence, in poverty and suffering, in persecution and contempt, in annihilation and the cross? The saints find him in heaven, in the splendors of glory, and in unspeakable pleasures, but only after having dwelt with him on earth in reproaches, in pain, and in humiliation. To be a Christian is to be an imitator of Jesus. In what can we imitate him if not in his humiliation? Nothing else can bring us near to him. We may adore him as omnipotent, fear him as just, love him with all our heart as good and merciful, but we can only imitate him as humble, submissive, poor, and despised.

Let us not imagine that we can do this by our own efforts. Everything in us is opposed to it; but we may rejoice that God is present within us. Jesus has chosen to be made partaker of all our weaknesses. He is a compassionate High Priest, who has voluntarily submitted to be tempted in all points as we are.[2] Let us, then, derive all our strength in him who became weak that he might strengthen us. Let us enrich ourselves out of his poverty, confidently exclaiming, "I can do everything through him who gives me strength."[3]

Let us earnestly occupy ourselves with this work, and let us change our hard hearts which are so rebellious, to become like the heart of Jesus Christ.

O lovely Jesus! You suffered so many injuries and reproaches for my sake. Let me cherish and love them for your sake, and help me desire to share your life of humiliation.

[1] Psalm 119:37 (KJV).
[2] Hebrews 4:15.
[3] Philippians 4:13 (NIV).

eight

The Uses of Humiliation

What a mercy is humiliation to a soul that receives it with steadfast faith! There are a thousand blessings in it for ourselves and for others, for our Lord bestows his grace upon the humble.

Humility makes us charitable toward our neighbor. Nothing will make us so generous and merciful to the faults of others as seeing our own.

Two things produce humility when they are put together: The first is the sight of the abyss of wretchedness from which the all-powerful hand of God has snatched us, and over which he still holds us, as it were, suspended in the air. The other is the presence of that God who is *All*.

Our faults, even those most difficult to bear, will all be of service to us, if we make use of them for our humiliation, without relaxing our efforts to correct them. It does no good to be discouraged. That is only the result of a disappointed and despairing self-love. The true method of profiting from the humiliation of our faults is to see them in all their deformity without losing our hope in God and without having any confidence in ourselves.

We must bear with ourselves without either flattery or discouragement, although we seldom achieve this happy median. We either expect great things of ourselves and of our good intentions, or else we wholly despair. We must hope for nothing from self, but wait for everything from God. Convicted of our helplessness, we have no confidence in ourselves, and yet we have unbounded confidence in God. These are the true foundations of the spiritual edifice.

Those who are truly humble will be surprised to hear anything exalted of themselves. They are calm and peaceful, of a contrite and humble heart, merciful and compassionate. They are quiet, cheerful, obedient, watchful, fervent in spirit, and incapable of strife. They always take the lowest place, rejoice when they are despised, and consider everyone better than themselves. They are lenient to the faults of others in view of their own and very far from preferring themselves before anyone. We may thus judge our progress in humility by the delight we have in humiliations and contempt.

nine

Bearing Our Faults Patiently

I pray God that he may preserve you in complete faithfulness to his grace. May he who began a good work in you bring it to completion at the day of Jesus Christ.[1] We must bear with ourselves patiently, without flattering ourselves, and we must continually subject ourselves to all that can overcome our natural inclinations and our inner dislikes, so that we may become more adaptable to the impressions of divine grace in living out the gospel.

This work, however, must be peaceful and untroubled. It must even be moderate, and we must not attempt to do all the work in a single day. We must try to reason little and to do much. If we do not take care, our whole life may be passed in reasoning, and we shall require a second life to practice! We run the risk of believing that we have advanced in proportion to our understanding of perfection. All these fine ideas, far from advancing us in dying to ourselves, may only serve to secretly nourish the life of the old Adam within us by giving us confidence in our own opinions. *Be extremely distrustful of your intellect and your own ideas of perfection.* That will be a great step toward becoming perfect. Humility and distrust of yourself, with simplicity, are fundamental virtues for you.

[1] Cf. Philippians 1:6.

ten

When Feelings Fail Us

Many are tempted to believe that they no longer pray when they cease to enjoy a certain pleasure in the act of prayer. But if they will remember that perfect prayer is only another name for love of God, their eyes will be open to the truth.

Prayer does not consist in sweet feelings, nor in the appeal of an excited imagination, nor in that illumination of mind that traces the sublimest truths in God with ease. It is not even in a certain consolation in our vision of God. All these things are external gifts from his hand. If they are withheld from us, our love may become more pure, as the soul may then attach itself immediately and solely to God instead of to his mercies.

This is that love by naked faith which is the death of

nature, because it leaves it no support. When we are convinced that all is lost, that very conviction is the evidence that all is gained.

Pure love is in the will alone. It is not sentimental love, for imagination has no part in it. It loves, if we may so express it, without feeling, as faith believes without seeing. We need not fear that this love is an imaginary thing. Nothing can be less so than the mere will when it is separated from all imagination. Without such emotional feeling, faith is in full exercise while humility is preserved.

Such love is chaste, for it is the love of God, in and for God. We are attached to him, but not for the pleasure which he bestows on us. We follow him, but not for the loaves and fishes.

Someone may indeed object that this "will" is a mere idea, a trick of the imagination instead of a true willing of the soul. I should indeed believe that it was a deception if it were not the parent of faithfulness on all proper occasions. A good tree brings forth good fruit, and a true will makes us truly earnest and diligent in doing the will of God. But it is still compatible in this life with little failings which are permitted by God that the soul may be humbled. If, then, we experience only these little daily frailties, let us not be discouraged, but extract their proper fruit from them.

True virtue and pure love reside in the will alone. Is it not a great matter always to desire the supreme good wherever he is seen, to keep our mind steadily turned toward him, and to bring it back whenever it wanders? Is it not a great thing to will nothing but that which is according to his order? In short, is it not a great matter to remain the same in the spirit of a yielded, irreclaimable burnt-offering when all earthly enjoyment is gone? Do you think it is nothing to deny all the uneasy reflections of self-love, and to press forward continually without knowing where we are headed—yet to go on without stopping? Is it a small thing to cut off satisfying thoughts of self, or at least to think of ourselves as we would of another, and to obey the Spirit's leadings for the moment without trying to look ahead?

It is a kind of betrayal of simple faith to continually demand to be assured that we are doing well. It is the will of God that we should be ignorant, and to reason about the way is to trifle along it. The safest and shortest course is to renounce, forget, and abandon the demands of self, and through faithfulness to God to think no more of such demands. This is what commitment means: to get out of self and self-love in order to get into God.

eleven

When We Feel
Abandoned by God

We should never so fully abandon ourselves to God as when he seems to abandon us. Let us enjoy light and consolation when it is his pleasure to give them to us, but let us not attach ourselves to his gifts, but to him. When he plunges us into the night of pure faith, let us still press on through agonizing darkness.

Moments are worth days in this tribulation. The soul is troubled and yet at peace. Not only is God hidden from it, but the soul is hidden from itself, that *all* may be of faith. The soul is discouraged but feels nevertheless an immovable will to bear all that God may choose to inflict. It wills all, accepts all, even the troubles that test its faith, and thus in the very height of the tempest, the waters beneath are secretly calm and at peace, because its will is one with God's will.

Blessed be the Lord who performs such great things in us, notwithstanding our unworthiness!

twelve

Living in the Present

One of the cardinal rules of the spiritual life is that we are to live in the present moment. You remember that the Israelites in the desert followed the pillar of fire or cloud, not knowing where it was leading them. They had a supply of manna but for one day, and any they gathered for the next day became useless.

There is no need to move in haste. Think only of laying a solid foundation. See that it is deep and broad by an absolute renunciation of self, and by abandonment without reserve to the requirements of God. Then let God raise upon this foundation such a building as he pleases. Shut your eyes and commit yourself to him. How wonderful is this walking with Abraham in pure faith, not knowing whither we go! And how full of blessings is the path!

God will be your Guide. He himself will travel with you, as we are told he did with the Israelites, to bring them step by step across the desert to the Promised Land. Ah! what will be your blessedness if you will but surrender yourself into the hands of God, permitting him to do whatever he will, not according to your desires, but according to his own good pleasure!

thirteen

On Pure Love

The LORD *hath made all things for himself,* says the Scripture.[1] Everything belongs to him, and he will never release his right to anything. Free and intelligent creatures are as much his as are those which are otherwise. He directs every unintelligent thing totally and absolutely to himself, and he desires that his intelligent creatures should voluntarily make the same disposition of themselves. It is true that he desires our happiness, but that is neither the chief end of his work, nor an end to be compared with that of his glory. It is for his glory only that he wills our happiness. Happiness is a subordinate consideration which he assigns to the final and essential end of his glory.

In order that we may align ourselves with his purpose in this respect, we must prefer God before ourselves, and we must seek to will our own happiness for his glory. In any other case, we invert the order of things. We must not desire his glory on account of our own salvation, but on the other hand, we should see that our own happiness is a thing which he has been pleased to make a part of his glory. It is true that all holy souls are not capable of exercising this explicit preference for God over themselves, but there must be at least an implicit preference.[2]

We human beings have a great distaste for this truth, and consider it to be a very hard saying, because we are lovers of self. We understand, in a general and superficial way, that we must love God more than all his creatures, but we have no conception of loving God more than ourselves, and loving ourselves only for him. We can utter these great words without difficulty, because we do not fully comprehend their meaning, but we shudder when it is explained to us that God and his glory are to be preferred before ourselves and everything else to such a degree that we must love his glory more than our own happiness, and must refer our happiness to his glory as merely a means to an end.

[1] Proverbs 16:4 (KJV).

[2] By this I understand Fénelon to mean that we cannot, except by a supernatural act of God's grace, *be happy* and feel good about this choice. We can, however, by an act of our will, give God permission to advance his glory, even at the cost of our happiness, trusting him to change our feelings in due time, in full assurance that our true happiness advances his glory.—*Ed.*

fourteen

The Refinements of Self-Love

The origin of our trouble is that we love ourselves with a blind passion that amounts to idolatry. If we love anything beyond, it is only for our own sakes. We must be undeceived about all those generous friendships in which it seems as though we have forgotten ourselves so far as to think only of the interests of our friend. If the motive of our friendship is not low and unrefined, it is nevertheless still selfish; and the more delicate, the more concealed, and the more proper such friendship is in the eyes of the world, the more dangerous it becomes, and the more likely to poison us by feeding our self-love.

In those friendships which appear so generous and unselfish, we seek the pleasure of loving without recompense. By indulging so noble a sentiment, we raise ourselves above the weak and sordid members of our race. Besides that tribute which we pay to our own pride, we seek from the world the reputation of unselfishness and generosity. We want to be loved by our friends even though we do not desire to be served by them. We hope that they will be pleased with what we do for them without expecting any return from them. In this way we get that very return which we seem to despise, for what is more delicious to a delicate self-love, than to hear itself applauded for not being self-love?

You may have seen someone who seemed to think of everyone but himself, who was the delight of good people, who was well disciplined and seemed entirely unmindful of self. This self-denial is so great that self-love would even imitate it, and find no glory equal to that of seeming to seek none at all. This moderation and self-renunciation which, if genuine, would be the death of the old natural self, becomes, on the other hand, the most subtle and imperceptible food of a pride that despises all ordinary forms of glory and desires only that glory which is to be secured by trampling all the unrefined objects of ambition that captivate ordinary minds.

It is not difficult to unmask this modest arrogance—this pride which seems not to be pride at all because it appears to have renounced all the ordinary objects of pride's ambition. Condemn it and it cannot bear to be found fault with. Let those whom it loves fail to repay it with friendship, esteem, and confidence, and it is stung to the quick! It is easy to see that it is not disinterested, though it tries so hard to seem so. It does not indeed accept payment in such gross coins as others may. It does not desire empty praise, or money, or that repayment which consists in office and dignities. It must be paid, nevertheless. It is greedy of the esteem of good people. It loves so that it may be loved in return and admired for its unselfishness. It *seems* to forget self, so that it may draw attention of the world upon self alone.

Of course it does not make all these reflections in full detail. It does not say in so many words, "I will deceive the whole world with my generosity in order that the world may love and admire me." Of course it would not dare address such unworthy language to itself! *It deceives itself along with everyone else.* It admires itself in its generosity, as a beautiful woman admires her beauty in a mirror. It is moved by thinking that it is more generous and unselfish than the rest of mankind. The illusion it prepares for others it extends to itself and this is what pleases it more than anything else.

However little we may have looked within ourselves to study the occasions of our pleasure and our grief, we shall have no more difficulty in admitting that pride has various tastes, whether it is more delicate or less so. But give it what taste you will, it is still pride, and that which appears the most restrained and the most reasonable is the most devilish. In esteeming itself, it despises others. It pities those who are pleased with foolish vanities. It recognizes the emptiness of greatness and rank. It cannot abide with those who are intoxicated with good fortune. It would, by its moderation, be *above* fortune, and thus raise itself to a new height by putting under foot all the false glory of man. Like Lucifer, it would become like the Most High. And it does not perceive that it seeks to place itself above others by this deceitful pride which blinds it.

We may be sure, then, that it is only the love of God that can make us come out of self. If his powerful hand did not sustain us, we should not know how to take the first step in that direction.

There is no middle course: we must refer everything either to God or to self. If we refer it to self, we have no god other than self. If we refer it to God, we are then in order, and regarding ourselves only as one among the other creatures of God, without selfish interests. With a single eye to accomplish his will, we enter into that self-abandonment which our Lord calls us to make.[1]

[1] Self-abandonment should be here understood only in the light of the Gospel word: "If anyone would come after me, he must deny himself, and take up his cross daily, and follow me" (St. Luke 9:23, NIV). And the word of our Lord, "Whoever finds his life will lose it, and whoever loses his life for my sake will find it" (St. Matthew 10:39, NIV; see also St. Matthew 16:25; St. Mark 8:35; St. Luke 9:24; St. John 12:25). There is no annihilation of identity or personhood, but the placing of our life—every part of it—under the Lordship of Christ.

fifteen

Listening to God
Rather than Self

You allow yourself to be led away too much by your inclination and your imagination. Apply yourself again to listen for the voice of God in prayer, and listen less to yourself. Self-love speaks less when it sees that we pay no attention to it.

The words of God to the heart are simple and peaceful; they nourish the soul, even if they bring death to it. On the contrary, the words of self-love are full of unevenness, of disturbance, and of emotion, even when they flatter us. To listen for the voice of God without making any plans of our own is to die to our own judgment and to our own will.

sixteen

The Miracle of Self-Denial

The greater our natural gift of frankness, the more we have pleasure in doing good, the more we love honor and generous friendship, the more we should distrust ourselves, and the more we should fear lest we take complacency in these natural gifts.

The reason why no created thing or person can draw us out of ourselves is that there is nothing on earth that deserves to be preferred before ourselves. There are none who have the right to claim such unqualified denial of self. Hence we love nothing outside our selves without the reference it has to our self-interest. If we are coarse and boorish, that will be the direction our self-love takes. If ours is a refined desire for glory, self cannot be satisfied with what is unrefined and vulgar.

But God does two things which only he has the power to do. He reveals himself to us, with all his rights over the creature and in all the appeals of his goodness. Then we feel that since we did not make ourselves, we are not made *for* ourselves. We begin to see that we were created for the glory of him who has been pleased to form us, and that he is too great to make anything except for himself. Thus we begin to realize that all our perfection and our happiness should be lost in him.

Created things, dazzling though they may be, cannot do this for us. Far from finding in them the infinity which so fills and satisfies us in God, we discover only a void, an inability to fill our hearts, an imperfection that continually drives us back into ourselves.

God's second miracle is to work in our hearts that which he pleases after he has enlightened our understanding. He is not satisfied with simply revealing his own charms. Rather, by his grace, he makes us love him by producing his love in our hearts. Thus he himself performs within us what he has caused us to see that we owe him.

There is little difficulty in comprehending that we must reject unlawful pleasures, dishonest gains, and unrefined vanities, because the very renouncement of these things involves a contempt that repudiates them absolutely and forbids us to derive any enjoyment from them. It is not, however, so easy to understand that we must abandon property honestly acquired, the pleasures of a modest and well-spent life, and the honors derived from a good reputation and a virtue that elevates us above the reach of envy.

The reason why we do not understand that these things must be given up is that we are not required to discard them with dislike. On the contrary, we are to preserve them to be used according to the responsibilities God places on us.

We need the consolation of a mild and peaceful life to console us under its troubles. As for honors, we are to regard that which is fitting. We must keep the property we possess to supply our needs. How then are we to renounce these things at the very moment we are occupied in preserving them? We are to make a sober use of them in moderation, without placing our hearts on them.

I say a *moderate use* of them, because when we are not attached to a thing for the purposes of self-enjoyment and of seeking our happiness in it, we use only as much of it as we need.

The abandonment of evil things, then, consists in refusing them with horror. The abandonment of good things consists in using them for our needs in moderation, continually seeking to refuse those *imaginary* needs with which greedy nature would flatter itself.

Remember that we must not only forsake evil, but also good things, for Jesus has said, "Whoever of you does not renounce all that he has cannot be my disciple."[1]

It follows then, that the Christian must forsake everything that he has, however innocent. For if we do not forsake it in our heart, it ceases to be innocent. This includes those things which it is our duty to guard with the greatest possible care, such as the good of our family, or our own reputation. We must not have our heart on any of these things. We must be ready to give them all up whenever it is the will of providence to deprive us of them.

Our renunciation of them consists in this: We are to love them for God only; to make use of the consolation of their love and friendship soberly, and for the supply of our needs; to be ready to part with them when God wills it. We should never seek in them the true repose of our heart. That is the chastity of true Christian friendship which seeks in the mortal and earthly friend only the heavenly Bridegroom. It is thus that we use the world and the things of creation without abusing them, according to St. Paul. He says, "Let . . . those who deal with the world [live] as though they had no dealings with it. For the form of this world is passing away."[2] We do not desire to take pleasure in them. We use only what God gives us, what he wills that we should love, with the reserve of a heart that is keeping itself for a more worthy Object.

It is in this sense that Christ would have us leave father and mother, brothers and sisters, and friends. It is in this sense that he comes to bring a sword upon earth.

God is a jealous God. If in the recesses of your soul, you are attached to any creature, your heart is not worthy of him. He must reject it as a bridegroom would reject a spouse who divided her affections between him and a stranger.

[1] St. Luke 14:33 (RSV).
[2] 1 Corinthians 7:31 (RSV).

seventeen

Bearing the Criticism of Others

Go on your spiritual journey naturally, and what others say will not harm you. A moderate, simple, decided course of conduct will impose silence upon them. Even if you have to bear some unkind mockeries, you will get off very cheaply. Having been approved by the world for so long, when you wished to please those who were blind, is it not just that you should have to suffer something from the folly of the world, so that you may acquire true wisdom? We are too jealous of a vain reputation when we fear the comments of those whom we do not admire and whose irregular conduct we know well. The main thing for you is to reserve to yourself hours for withdrawal, when by your exercise of devotion you can provide yourself with a good antidote against all their poisonous errors.

Read the truth in the words of eternal life. Pray, watch, and be detached from yourself. Love God with a generous love; let that which was created only for him belong only to him. Expect all things from him without neglecting yourself, that you may be faithful to his gifts.

After saying all this, you can see by the language which this letter contains, how much I am interested in all that concerns you.

eighteen

Meeting Temptations

I know of but two resources against temptations. One is
faithfully to follow the interior light, instantly and immediately cutting off everything that we are at liberty to dismiss
which may excite or strengthen temptation. I say everything
which we are at liberty to dismiss, because we are not always
permitted to avoid the occasions of evil. Those that are
unavoidably connected with the particular position in which
providence has placed us are not within our power to dismiss.

The other resource against temptation consists in turning
to God whenever temptation comes, without being disturbed
or anxious to know if we have not already yielded a sort of
half consent, and without interrupting our immediate
recourse to God. By examining too closely whether we have

not been guilty of some unfaithfulness, we incur the risk of being again entangled in the temptation. The shortest and surest way is to act like a little child at its mother's breast. When we show it a frightful monster, it shrinks back and buries its face in its mother's bosom, that it may no longer behold it.

The sovereign remedy is the habit of dwelling continually in the presence of God. He sustains, consoles, and calms us.

We must never be astonished at temptations, however outrageous they may be. On this earth all is temptation. Crosses tempt us by irritating our pride, while prosperity tempts us by flattering it. Our life is a continual combat, but one in which Jesus Christ fights for us. We must pass on unmoved while temptations rage around us, as the traveler, overtaken by a storm, simply wraps his cloak more closely about him and pushes on more vigorously toward his destined home.

If the thought of former sins and wretchedness should be permitted to come before us, we must remain confounded and abashed before God, quietly enduring in his adorable presence all the shame and ignominy of our transgressions. We must not, however, seek to entertain or to call up so dangerous a recollection.

In conclusion, it may be said that in doing what God wills there is very little to be done by us. And yet, there is a wonderful work to be accomplished; it is nothing less than that of keeping nothing back, making no resistance, even for a moment, to that jealous Love which searches inexorably into the most secret recesses of the soul for the smallest trace of self, for the slightest intimations of an affection of which Divine Love is not the Author. On the other hand, true progress does not consist in a multitude of self-searching, nor of austerities, troubles, and strife. It means simply to will nothing of self and everything of God, cheerfully performing each day's round as God appoints it for us, seeking nothing, refusing nothing, finding everything in the present moment, and allowing God, who does everything, to do his pleasure in and by us without the slightest resistance on our part.

Oh, how happy is the person who has attained this state! How full of good things is that soul, when it appears to be emptied of everything!

Let us pray the Lord to open to us the whole infinitude of his fatherly heart, that our own may be submerged and lost there, so that it may be as one with his. Such was the desire of St. Paul for the faithful, when he longed for them "with the affection of Christ Jesus" (Phil. 1:8 NIV).

nineteen

The Giver or the Gifts?

The best rule we can ever adopt is to receive with the same submission everything that God sends us, both within and from without.

There are many things in our circumstances which must be met with courage, and things pleasant that must not be allowed to capture our affections. We resist the temptations of the disagreeable by accepting them at once, and the temptations of the pleasant by refusing to admit them into our hearts.

This same course is necessary in regard to our interior life. Whatever is bitter serves to crucify us and works all its benefit in our souls if we receive it simply and with a willingness that knows no bounds, and with a readiness that seeks no alleviation.

Pleasant gifts, which are intended to support our weakness by giving us conscious consolation in our outward activities, must be accepted with equal satisfaction, but in a different way. They must be received because God sends them, rather than because they are agreeable to our own feelings. They are to be used like any other medicine, without self-complacency, without attachment to them, and without taking them for our own. We must accept them, but not hold on to them, so that when God sees fit to withdraw them, we may be neither dejected nor discouraged.

The root of presumption lies in our attachment to these passing and material gifts. We imagine we have no regard to anything but to the gift of God, while we are really looking to self, taking as our own possession his mercy and mistaking it for himself. Thus we become discouraged when we find that we have been deceived in ourselves. The soul that is sustained by God, however, is not surprised at its own wretchedness. It is delighted to find new proof that it can do nothing of itself and that God must do everything. We are never in the least troubled at being poor when we know that our Father has infinite treasures which he will give us. We will soon become free of trust in ourselves if we allow our hearts to feed upon absolute confidence in God.

We must count less on sensible delights and the measures of wisdom which we devise for our own perfection. We must count more upon simplicity, lowliness, renunciation of our own efforts, and our perfect pliability to all the designs of grace. Everything else tends to focus on *our* virtues and thus inspires a secret reliance on our own resources.

Let us pray God that he will root out of our hearts everything of *our* planting, and set there, with his own hands, the Tree of Life, bearing all manner of fruits.

twenty

When Undergoing Great Weakness

You are in God's hands. You must live as if you were to die each day. Then you will be quite ready, for our preparation for death simply consists in detaching ourselves from the world to attach ourselves to God.

While you are so weak, do not put the constraint upon yourself of making your prayer time so regularly.[1] Such exactitude and such application of mind might do harm to your feeble health. It is quite enough for you in your present state of weakness, if you again place yourself in the presence of God when you perceive that you are no longer there. A simple and familiar companionship with God, in which you can tell him all your troubles with perfect trust in him, and in which you can ask him to comfort and strengthen you, will never exhaust you. It will nourish your heart.

[1] The recipient of this letter was undergoing an undisclosed illness.

twenty-one

The Interior Voice
of the Spirit

It is certain from the Holy Scriptures that the Spirit of God dwells within us. There he acts, there he prays without ceasing, groans, desires, and asks for us what we do not know how to ask for ourselves. The Spirit urges us on, animates us, speaks to us when we are silent, suggests to us all truth, and so unites us to him that we become one spirit.[1] This is the teaching of faith, and even those teachers farthest removed from the interior life cannot avoid acknowledging it to be so. To be sure, there are some who strive to maintain that in practice, we are illuminated by the external law, or by the light of learning and reason, and that then our understanding acts of itself from that instruction. They do not rely sufficiently upon the interior Teacher, the Holy Spirit, who does everything within us. We could not form a thought or desire without him. Alas! what blindness is ours! We suppose ourselves alone in the inner sanctuary, when God is more intimately present there than we are ourselves.

You may say, "What then! Are we all inspired?" Yes, without a doubt! But not in the same way the prophets and apostles were. Without the actual inspiration of the Spirit of grace, we could neither do, nor will, nor believe any good thing. We are, then, always inspired, but we incessantly stifle the inspiration. God does not cease to speak, but the noise of the world outside us, and the noise of our passions within, prevent our hearing him. We must silence every creature, including self, that we may perceive the ineffable voice of the Bridegroom in the deep stillness of the soul. We must lend an attentive ear, for his voice is soft and still, and is heard only by those who hear nothing else!

How rare it is to find a soul still enough to hear God speak! The slightest murmur of our vain desires, or of a love fixed upon self, confounds all the words of the Spirit of God. We hear well enough that he is speaking and that he is asking for something, but we cannot distinguish what is said, and often we are glad enough that we cannot. The least reserve, the slightest act rooted in self-consideration, the most imperceptible fear of hearing too clearly what God demands interferes with the still, small voice.

Is it any wonder, then, that many people, religious people, are full of false wisdom, amusements, vain desires, and confidence in their own virtues, and that they cannot hear the voice of the Spirit within? Do we need be surprised that they consider its very possibility as a dream of fanatics? What good would be the spoken word of pastors and preachers, or even of the Scriptures themselves, if we did not have within the word of the Holy Spirit giving to those other words all their life and vitality? The spoken word, even of the gospel, without the life-giving interior word of the Spirit is but an empty sound. "For the letter kills," and the Spirit alone can give life.[2]

O eternal and omnipotent Word of the Father, it is you who speak in the depth of our soul.

The words that proceeded from the mouth of our Savior during the days of his mortal life have had energy to produce such wondrous fruits only because they have been animated by that Spirit of life which is the Word itself. Hence it is that St. Peter says, "Lord, to whom shall we go? You have the words of eternal life."[3]

It is not the outward law of the gospel alone that God shows us by the light of reason and faith. It is his Spirit within us who speaks, touches, operates in, and animates us. So it is the Spirit who does in us and with us whatever we do that is good, just as it is our soul that gives life to the body and regulates all its movements.

It is true that we are continually inspired and that we do not lead a gracious life except so far as we act under this inward inspiration. But alas! how few Christians feel it! How few are they who do not annihilate it by their voluntary distractions or by their resistance!

God is continually speaking to us.[4] He speaks to the unrepentant also, but, stunned by the noise of the world and their passions, they cannot hear him. The interior voice to them seems to be a fable.

He speaks to awakened sinners, and they feel remorse of conscience, which is the voice of God inwardly reproaching them for their sins. When they are deeply moved, they have no difficulty in understanding this inner voice, for it is this voice which pierces them so sharply. It is to them that "two-edged sword" of which St. Paul speaks as "piercing even to the dividing asunder of soul and spirit."[5] God causes himself to be perceived, enjoyed, and followed. They hear that sweet voice that sends a reproach to the bottom of the heart and causes it to be torn to pieces. Such is true and pure contrition.

God speaks, too, to wise and enlightened persons, whose life, outwardly correct, seems adorned with many virtues. But such are often too full of themselves and their own lights to listen to God. Everything is turned into reasoning. They substitute the principles of natural wisdom and the plans of human prudence for what would come infinitely better through the channel of simplicity and a willingness to be taught by the Word of God. They seem good, sometimes better than others, and they are so, perhaps, up to a certain point, but it is a mixed goodness. They are still in possession of themselves and always want to be so. They love to be in the hands of their own counsel and to be strong and great in their own eyes.

I thank you, O my God, with Jesus Christ, that you hid your ineffable secrets from these great and wise ones. You take pleasure in revealing them to feeble and humble souls! It is with babes alone that you are wholly unreserved; the others you treat in their own way. They desire knowledge and great virtues, and you give them dazzling illuminations and convert them into heroes. But this is not the better part. There is something more hidden for your dearest children. They lie with John on your breast. As for these great ones who are constantly afraid of becoming lowly, you leave them in all their greatness; they shall never share your caresses and your familiarity, for to deserve these, they must become as little children and play upon your knees.

[1] 1 Corinthians 6:17.

[2] 2 Corinthians 3:6 (NRSV).

[3] St. John 6:68 (RSV).

[4] *Imitation of Christ*, III, 2a: "I taught the prophets from the beginning, saith the Lord, and cease not, even to this day, to speak to all; but many are hardened and deaf to my voice."

[5] Hebrews 4:12 (KJV).

twenty-two

Judge Cautiously

In all things judge as little as you possibly can. It is a very simple matter to hold back all decisions that are not necessary for us. This is not irresolution. It is a simple distrust of ourselves and a very practical detachment from our own ideas, which extends to everything, even to the commonest things.

When we are truly detached, we believe what we ought to believe and we act when necessary with a simple determination and without reflection upon ourselves or trusting to ourselves. When there is no necessity, we do not judge, and we allow all appearances and all reasons for believing to pass before our eye, but we are so empty of self and of our own opinions that we are always ready to receive light from others. We are willing to believe that we are mistaken, and ready to retrace our steps like a little child whom its mother leads back by the hand.

This emptiness of spirit, this childlike docility will bring peace to your heart—peace with yourself and with your neighbor.

twenty-three

The Last Shall Be First

I have often observed that a rude, ignorant sinner, just beginning to be touched by a lively sense of the love of God, is much more disposed to listen to the inward language of the Spirit of grace than those enlightened and learned persons who have grown old in their own wisdom. God's sole desire is to impart himself. He cannot, so to speak, find where to set his foot in souls so full of themselves, who have grown fat upon their own wisdom and virtues. But, as the Scriptures say, "His secret is with the simple."[1]

But where are they? I do not know who they are, but God sees them and loves to dwell in them. "My Father and I," says our Lord Jesus Christ, "will come unto him, and make our home with him."[2] Ah! a soul delivered from self, and abandoned to grace, counting itself as nothing, walking without its own thought, moving at the will of that pure love which is its perfect Guide—that soul has an experience which the wise can neither receive nor understand!

I was once as wise as any. Thinking I saw everything I saw nothing. I crept along, feeling my way by a succession of reasonings, but there was no ray to enlighten my darkness. I was content to reason. But when we have silenced everything within us in order to listen to God, we know all things without knowing anything. Then we perceive that before this had taken place, we were utterly ignorant of all we thought we understood. We lose all that we once had, and do not care for it, because we have then nothing else that belongs to self. Everything is lost, and ourselves with it. There is something within us that joins with the spouse in the Song of Solomon in saying, "Show me your face, let me hear your voice; for your voice is sweet and your face is lovely."[3] Ah! how sweet is that voice; it makes me tremble within! Speak, O Beloved! and let none other dare to speak but you. Be still, my soul! Speak, Love!

Then it is that *we know all things without knowing anything*. Not that we have the presumption to suppose that we possess within ourselves all truth. No! On the contrary, we feel that we see nothing, can do nothing, and are nothing *in ourselves*. We feel it and are delighted at it. But in this state we find everything we need from moment to moment in the infinity of God. There we find the daily bread of knowledge and of everything else, without laying up. Then the unction from above teaches us all truth, while it takes away our own wisdom, glory, self-interest, even our own willfulness; it makes us content with our weakness and with a position below every creature. We are ready to yield to the lowest, and to confess our most secret wretchedness before the whole world, fearing unfaithfulness more than punishment and shame of face.

Here it is that the Spirit teaches us all truth: for all truth is inherently contained in this sacrifice of love, where the soul strips itself of everything to present it to God.

---

[1] Proverbs 3:32, Vulgate. His meaning is, "His secret dwelling place is with the simple."

[2] St. John 14:23 (NIV).

[3] Song of Solomon 2:14 (NIV).

twenty-four

When Spiritually Disheartened

It is indeed good to see only the friends whom God gives us, and to be protected from all the rest! In the midst of my difficulties I often feel inclined to sigh after that liberty which solitude brings. But we must stay in the path marked out for us, and go on our way without listening to our own preferences.

Avoid weariness, and give some satisfaction to your natural activity. Seek a certain number of persons whose company is not disagreeable to you and who can refresh your mind when there is need of it. We do not need a great deal of company, and we must accustom ourselves not to be too particular. It is sufficient if we find some good people who are quiet and moderately reasonable. Vary your occupations so that you may not be fatigued with any one of them.

I am not at all surprised that your feelings of lukewarmness and your lack of attraction to the spiritual life should cast you down. Nothing can be more disheartening. You have only two things to do, it seems to me: One is to avoid all that distracts or absorbs you. By doing this you will cut off the source of everything that can be a dangerous distraction and can dry up your prayer. We must not expect to be nourished within when we are always taken up with external things. Faithfulness in renouncing things that make you too excited and too unreserved in conversation is absolutely necessary to draw down upon yourself the spirit of tranquillity and prayer. We cannot enjoy God and the world at the same time. We keep regular in our prayers and for two hours keep the same disposition that we have in our hearts during the rest of the day.

Having cut off the things that distract you, you must try frequently to renew your sense of the presence of God, even in the midst of the things which are necessary for you, so that you may not throw into them too much of your purely natural action. You must try to act always by grace in the spirit of death to self. We can gradually arrive at this by often suspending our impulsiveness, to listen to the voice of God within the soul, and to let him take possession of us.

twenty-five

Dealing with Our Faults

Many of our faults are voluntary in different degrees, though they may not be committed with a deliberate purpose of failing God. One friend sometimes reproaches another for a fault not expressly intended to offend, and yet committed with the knowledge that it would do so. In the same way, God lays this sort of fault to our charge. They are voluntary, for although not done with an express intention, they are still committed freely and against a certain inner light of conscience, which should have caused us to hesitate and wait. Godly souls are often guilty of these offenses. As for those committed deliberately, it would be strange indeed if a soul consecrated to God should fall into such.

Little faults become great and even monstrous in our eyes, to the extent that we increase in the pure light of God. Just as the rising sun reveals the true size of objects which were seen dimly during the night, the increase of inward light will show our imperfections to be far greater and more deadly in their roots than we had thought them. We witness, in addition, a host of other faults, of whose existence we had not the slightest suspicion. We find the weaknesses necessary to deprive us of all confidence in our own strength. This discovery, however, far from discouraging us, serves to destroy our self-reliance and to raze to the ground the edifice of pride. Nothing marks so decidedly the solid progress of a soul as being able to view its own depravity without being disturbed or discouraged.

It is an important precept to abstain from doing a wrong thing whenever we perceive it in time, and when we do note that we have done it, to bear the humiliation of the fault courageously. If a fault is perceived before it is committed, we must see to it that we do not resist and quench the Spirit of God warning us of it inwardly. The Spirit is easily offended and very jealous. He desires to be listened to and obeyed. He retires if he is displeased. The slightest resistance to him is a wrong, for everything must yield to him the moment he is perceived. Faults of haste and frailty are nothing compared with those of shutting our ears when the voice of the Holy Spirit begins to speak in the depths of the heart.

Restlessness and an injured self-love will never mend those faults which are not recognized until after they are committed. On the contrary, such feelings are simply the impatience of wounded pride at beholding what confounds it. We must quietly humble ourselves in peace. I say *humble ourselves in peace,* for there is no humiliation if we do it in a vexed and spiteful way. We must condemn our faults, mourn over them, and repent of them without seeking the slightest shadow of consolation in any excuse. We must behold ourselves covered with shame in the presence of God, and all this without being bitter against ourselves or discouraged, but peacefully reaping the profit of our humiliation. In this way we draw from the serpent itself the antidote of his venom.

It often happens that what we offer to God is not what he most desires to have of us. *That* we are frequently the most unwilling to give, and the most fearful that he will ask. He desires the sacrifice of *Isaac*, the well-beloved son. All the rest is as nothing in his eyes, and he permits it all to be offered in a painful, unprofitable manner, because he has no blessings for a divided soul. He will have everything, and until then there is no rest. "Who has resisted him and come out unscathed?"[1] Would you prosper and secure the blessing of God upon your labors? Reserve nothing, cut to the quick and burn, spare nothing, and the God of peace will be with you! What consolation, what liberty, what strength, what enlargedness of heart, what increase of grace will follow when there remains nothing between God and the soul, and when the last sacrifices have been offered up without hesitation!

We must be neither astonished nor disheartened. We are not more wicked than we were. We are really less so, but while our evil diminishes, our light increases, and we are struck with horror at its extent. But let us remember, for our consolation, that the perception of our disease is the first step in its cure. When we have no sense of our need, we have no curative principle within. It is a state of blindness, presumption, and insensibility, in which we are delivered over to our own counsel, and commit ourselves to the current whose fatal speed we do not realize until we are called to struggle against it.

We must not be discouraged either, by our weakness or by dislike of the constant activity which may be a part of our life. Discouragement is not the fruit of humility, but of pride. Nothing can be worse. Suppose we have stumbled, or even fallen. Let us rise and run again. All our falls are useful if they strip us of a disastrous confidence in ourselves, while they do not take away a humble and saving trust in God.

The dislikes we feel toward our duties come from our imperfections. If we were perfect and mature, we should love everything in the order of God. Since we are born corrupt, however, and with a nature revolting against his laws, let us praise him that he knows how to bring good from evil, and can use even our dislikes as a source of virtue. The work of grace does not always progress as evenly as that of nature, says St. Teresa.

Carefully purify your conscience, then, from daily faults. Allow no sin to dwell in your heart. Small as it may seem, it obscures and dims the light of grace, weighs down the soul, and hinders that constant communion with Jesus Christ which it should be your pleasure to cultivate. You will become lukewarm, forget God, and find yourself growing in attachment to the world. A pure soul, on the other hand, which is humiliated and rises promptly after its smallest faults, remains fervent and upright.

God never makes us aware of our weakness except to give us his strength. Do not be disturbed by what is not deliberate. The great point is, never to act in opposition to the inward light, and to be willing to go as far as God would have us go.

[1] Job 9:4.

twenty-six

Faithfulness in Small Things

St. Francis de Sales says that great virtues and faithfulness in small things are like sugar and salt. Sugar is more delicious, but of less frequent use, while salt enters into every article of our food. Great virtues are rare. They are seldom needed, and when the occasion comes, we are prepared for it by everything which has gone before. We are excited by the greatness of the sacrifice involved, and sustained, either by the brilliancy of the action in the eyes of others, or by self-confidence in our ability to do such wonderful things.

Small occasions, however, are unforeseen. They recur every moment and place us constantly in conflict with our pride, our laziness, our self-esteem, and our passions. They are calculated thoroughly to subdue our wills, and leave us no retreat. If we are faithful in them, the old nature will have no time to breathe. It must die to all its inclinations. It would please us much better to make some great sacrifices, however painful and violent, on the condition that we could then be free to follow our own pleasure and to keep our old habits in little things. It is, however, only by faithfulness in small matters that the grace of true love is sustained and distinguished from the fleeting excitements of a purely human nature.

We may compare the godly life with our temporal goods: there is more danger from the little expenses than from larger expenditures, and he who understands how to take care of little things will soon accumulate more. Everything great owes its greatness to the small elements that compose it. He that loses nothing soon will be rich.

Consider, on the other hand, that God does not so much regard our actions as he does the motive of love from which they spring and the pliability of our wills to his. Men judge our deeds by their outward appearance; with God, that which is most dazzling in the eyes of man is of no account. What he desires is a pure intention, a will ready for anything, and ever pliable in his hands. What he seeks is the giving up of self. All this can be manifested much more frequently on small occasions than on extraordinary ones. There will also be much less danger from pride, and the test will be far more searching. Indeed, it sometimes happens that we find it harder to part with a trifle than with an important interest. It may be more of a cross to us to abandon a vain amusement than to give a large gift to charity.

We are more easily deceived about small matters if we imagine them to be innocent and think that we are indifferent to them. Nevertheless, when God takes them away we may easily recognize, in the pain of their loss, how excessive was our use of them and how inexcusable was our attachment to them. If we are in the habit of neglecting little things, we shall be constantly offending our families, our fellow workers, and all who are related to us. No one can well believe that our Christian walk is sincere when our behavior is careless and irregular in its little details. What ground have we for believing that we are ready to make the greatest sacrifices if we daily fail in offering the least?

The greatest danger of all is this: by neglecting small matters, our soul becomes accustomed to unfaithfulness. We grieve the Holy Spirit. We revert to ourselves. We begin to think it a small thing to be lacking towards God. On the other hand, true love can see nothing as small; everything that can either please or displease God seems to be great. It is not that true love disturbs the soul with scruples,[1] but it puts no limits to its faithfulness. It acts simply with God, and as it does not concern itself about those things which God does not require from it, so it never hesitates an instant about those things he does, whether they are great or small.

Thus it is not by incessant care that we become faithful in the smallest things, but simply by a love which is free from the reflections and fears of a restless and overscrupulous soul. We are, as it were, drawn along by the love of God. We have no desire to do anything but what we do, no will regarding anything which we do or do not do. At the very moment when God is following the soul, relentlessly pursuing it into the smallest details and seemingly taking away all its freedom, the soul finds itself in a spacious place and enjoys a perfect peace in him. Happy soul!

Those who are by nature less strict in small matters should lay down and preserve inviolate the most rigid laws respecting them. They are tempted to despise small things, habitually thinking them unimportant. They do not understand the unconscious and hidden progress of our emotions, and even forget their own sad experience on that subject. They prefer to be deluded by the promise of an imaginary future firmness, and to trust to their own courage that has so often deceived them, rather than to subject themselves to unceasing faithfulness. "It is a small matter," they say. That is true, but it is of amazing consequence to you. It is something you love enough to refuse to give it up to God. It is something you sneer at in words, so that you may have an excuse to keep it: a small matter—but one that you withhold from your Maker, which can prove your ruin.

It is not nobility of the soul that despises small things. On the contrary, it is a constricted, shrunken spirit that regards as unimportant what it cannot project to its inevitable result. The more it causes us to be on our guard against small matters, the more we need to fear negligence, to distrust our strength, and to put impregnable barriers between ourselves and the smallest carelessness.

Finally, judge by your own feelings. What would you think of a friend who owed everything to you and who was willing from a sense of duty to serve you on those rare occasions which are called great, but who should manifest neither affection nor the least regard for your wishes in the common, everyday things of life?

Do not be frightened at this attention to small matters. It takes courage at first, but this is a discipline which you need, and it will yield you peace and security. Without it, all is trouble and relapse. God will gradually make it pleasant and easy to you, for true love is obedient without constraint, and without strife or effort.

---

[1] It is very important that a word of caution be sounded here against taking this chapter as a justification for scrupulous concern for little things. It is the mark of immature and self-righteous spirituality which becomes anxious about little things and neglects the great ones. Fénelon's word here is spoken to those who excuse themselves in the little things, not to those who are already plagued with the fear of being wrong. Cf. Chapter 4 in *The Royal Way of the Cross* and my note on *Scruples* there. —Ed.

twenty-seven

Exactitude and
Liberty of Spirit

We should unite a great exactitude with a great liberty. Exactitude will make you faithful, and liberty will make you courageous. If you were to attempt to be exact without being free, you would fall into slavery and scruples. If you were to attempt to be free without being exact, you would soon degenerate into negligence and carelessness. Exactitude by itself narrows the mind and heart, and liberty by itself loosens them too much.

Those who have no experience in the ways of God do not believe that these two virtues can agree together. They think that being exact means always living under constraint, in distress of mind, in an uneasy and scrupulous timidity which robs the soul of all its rest and makes it see sins everywhere. They think that being exact hampers the soul so much that it is in constant conflict with itself about everything—down to the merest trifles, scarcely daring to breathe. To be free, they say, is to have a wide conscience, and not to pay too close an attention even to that, to be satisfied with avoiding gross faults, and to count as considerable faults only gross crimes. Excepting only these, they allow themselves everything that can artfully flatter self-love. Whatever license we may give to our passions, we are to calm and console ourselves easily by the simple thought that we did not see any great evil in such things. St. Paul did not speak in this way when he said to those whom he had brought into the life of grace and of whom he was trying to make perfect Christians: *Be free, but with the liberty which Jesus Christ has purchased for you; be free, because the Savior has called you to freedom; but do not let this liberty be for you an occasion or a pretext for doing evil.*[1]

True exactitude consists in obeying God in all things. It means to follow the light that shows us our duty and the grace that urges us to do it, having for the principle of our conduct the desire to please God in all things and always to do, not only that which is agreeable to him, but if possible, that which is *most* agreeable to him without bothering ourselves with quibbling about the difference between great sins and little sins, between imperfections and infidelities. For, although it is true that there is a difference between all these things, there ought to be no such distinction any longer for a soul that is determined to refuse nothing to God that it can give him. It is in this sense that the Apostle says that "the law is not made for the righteous man,"[2]—the constraining law, the hard law, the threatening law, if we may dare to say so, the tyrannical and enslaving law. But the just man has a superior law which raises him above all that and which makes him enter into the true liberty of the children of God;

that is, always to wish to do that which is most pleasing to his heavenly Father, according to those excellent words of St. Augustine: "Love, and then do what you will."

To a sincere will always to do that which seems best to us in the sight of God, we may unite the further intention of doing it with joy, of never allowing ourselves to be discouraged when we have not done it. We may begin over and over again, hundreds of times, resolved to do it better, hoping always that in the end we *shall* do it, bearing with ourselves in our unintentional weaknesses as God bears with us. We can wait patiently for the moment that he has marked out for our perfect deliverance, making up our mind meanwhile to walk on with simplicity in the way that is open to us, according to our strength, not losing time in looking behind us. We are to extend our energies and set our faces steadily always, as the Apostle says, "to the things which lie before us,"[3] not making a multitude of useless reflections upon our failures, which would only keep us back, trouble our minds, and cast down our heart. We must humble ourselves for them, grieving over them when we first see them, but afterwards we must leave them and go on our way. We are not to interpret everything against ourselves with a literal and legalistic severity, looking upon God as a spy who is watching us so that he may surprise us, or as an enemy who is laying snares for us, but rather as a Father who loves us and wishes to save us. If we persevere in these intentions, and are full of confidence in his goodness, careful to invoke his mercy, and are rid of all our vain reliance on creatures and on ourselves—if we do all this, we shall have found the way to true and perfect liberty, and perhaps its fixed dwelling place.

Aspire to this. Exactitude and liberty ought to walk together with even steps. But indeed I think you have more need to lean to the side of confidence in God and a great expansion of heart. It is for this reason that I do not hesitate in telling you that you must give yourself up entirely to the grace that God gives you sometimes in a close union with himself. Do not fear at such times to lose sight of yourself, to contemplate him alone and as closely as he will allow you to do so. Don't be afraid to plunge yourself in the ocean of his love. Happy you, if you could do it so perfectly as never to find yourself again! It is good, when God gives you this grace, to finish always with an act of humility and of filial and respectful fear. This will prepare your soul for new gifts. This is the advice of St. Teresa, and I commend it to you.

[1] Paraphrase of Galatians 5:13.
[2] 1 Timothy 1:9.
[3] Philippians 3:13.

twenty-eight

Dealing with Contradictory Feelings

We must not be surprised if we frequently find in ourselves emotions of pride, of self-complacency, of self-confidence, of desire to follow our own inclination against what is right, of impatience at the weakness of others, or even of annoyance at our own state. In such cases we must instantly let them drop like some stone to the bottom of the sea, place ourselves again in God, and before acting, wait until we are in such a frame of heart as our recollection can bring forth in us. If the distraction of business, or of tenacity of imagination, should keep us from entering calmly and easily into such a state, we must at least try to be quiet by a steady set of the will and by the desire for such refocusing. In such case, the will to be recollected serves to deprive the soul of its own will and to render it submissive in the hands of God.

If in your excitement, some emotion too nearly like the old fallen nature should come up in you, do not be discouraged. Go straight on. Quietly bear the humiliation of your fault before God without allowing self-love to smart at the betrayal of its weakness. Proceed confidently, without being troubled by the anguish of a wounded pride that cannot bear to see itself imperfect. Your fault will be of service in causing you to die to self and to become nothing before him.

The true method of curing this defect is to become dead to the sensitiveness of self-love, without impeding the movement of grace, which had been slightly interrupted by this fleeting unfaithfulness!

The great point is to renounce your own wisdom by honesty of conduct, and to be ready to give up the favor, esteem, and approval of everyone whenever the path in which God leads you requires it.

We are not to meddle with things which God does not lay upon us, nor uselessly utter hard sayings which those about us are not able to bear. We must follow after God, never go before him. When he gives the signal, we must leave all and follow him. If we hesitate, delay, lose courage, and dilute what he would have us do; if we indulge fears for our own comfort or safety, desiring to shield ourselves from suffering and bad repute; or if we seek to find some excuse for not performing a difficult and painful duty, we are truly guilty in his sight, especially so after we have made an absolute consecration and a conviction in conscience that he is requiring something of us. May God keep us from such unfaithfulness! Nothing is more dreadful than this inward resistance to him.

Other faults committed in the simplicity of your good intention will be of service if they produce humility and make you of less and less account in your own eyes. But resistance to the Spirit of God through pride or a cowardly worldly wisdom, concerned for its own comfort in performing the work of God, is a fault which will imperceptibly quench the Spirit of grace in your heart. God, jealous and rejected after so much mercy, will depart and leave you to your own resources. You will then turn around in a kind of circle instead of advancing with rapid strides along the King's highway. Your inward life will grow dim and dimmer, without your being able to detect the sure and deep-seated source of your disease.

God would choose to behold in us a singleness which can contain as much more of his wisdom as it contains less of our own. He desires to see us lowly in our own eyes, and as meek in his hands as a little child. He desires to create in our heart the childlike disposition so distasteful to the spirit of fallen man, but so agreeable to the spirit of the gospel.

By this very singleness and lowliness he will heal all the remnants of haughty and self-confident wisdom in us, and we shall say with David, *I will make myself more undignified than this, and I will be humiliated in my own eyes,*[1] from the moment we give ourselves to the Lord.

[1] 2 Samuel 6:22 (NIV).

twenty-nine

Maintaining Faith
Without Feelings

You rely a little too much on the concentration of your soul and feelings in the presence of God. God has taken away these sensible gifts to detach you from them, to teach you how weak you are of yourself, and to accustom you to serve God without that enjoyment which makes virtue easy. The same service is much more to him when we perform it without pleasure and with distaste. I do very little for my friend when I go to see him, walking on foot, because I love walking, have excellent legs, and take a very great pleasure in using them. But if I become gouty, then every step that I take costs me a great deal of pain, and so the same visits that I formerly made to my friend, and which he did not think much of, begin to have a new value. They become signs of a very deep and very strong friendship, and the more pain I have in making them, the more he appreciates it. One step taken in that pain is more meritorious than a hundred steps in pleasure.

I say this to prevent you from falling into a very dangerous temptation, which is discouragement and trouble. When you are enjoying the abundance of grace and interior fervor, then count all your good works as nothing, because they flow, so to speak, from the very Source. But, on the contrary, when you feel yourself to be in dryness, obscurity, poverty, and almost powerlessness of soul, remain humble under the hand of God in a state of bare faith, recognize your own misery, turn yourself toward the all-powerful Lord, and never doubt his assistance. Oh, how good it is for us to see ourselves stripped of all those emotional supports that flatter self-love and reduced to confess the truth of those words of Holy Scripture, "No one living is righteous before you."[1]

Walk on always, in the name of God, although it may seem to you that you have neither strength nor courage to put one foot in front of the other. If human courage fails you, so much the better. If you abandon yourself to God, he will not fail to help your powerlessness. St. Paul exclaims, "When I am weak, then I am strong." And when he prayed to be delivered from his weakness, God answered him, "My power is made perfect in weakness."[2] Allow yourself, then, to be made perfect by experiencing your imperfection and by humbly fleeing to him who is the strength of the weak.

When you are in prayer, engage yourself, with a simple freedom, with all that can help you to pray and that will help you to remain focused. Relieve your imagination which is sometimes impatient, and sometimes exhausted. Make use of everything that can calm it and help you to an informal communication with God. All that is to your taste and according to your needs in this loving conversation will be good. "Where the Spirit of the Lord is, there is freedom."[3] This innocent and simple liberty consists in seeking simply and honestly the nourishment of love that can most easily unite us with the Beloved of our soul. Your inner poverty will often recall you to a feeling of your misery. God, who is so good, will not allow you to lose sight of how unworthy you are of him, and the thought of your own unworthiness will bring you back at once to his infinite goodness.

Take courage! The work of God can only be done by the destruction of the self-life. May he sustain you, comfort you, make you poor, and help you experience the truth of that beautiful word, "Blessed are the poor in spirit."[4]

[1] Psalm 143:2 (NIV).
[2] 2 Corinthians 12:10, 9 (NIV).
[3] 2 Corinthians 3:17 (NIV).
[4] St. Matthew 5:3.

thirty

Undue Attachment
to Feelings

Those who are committed to God only so far as they enjoy pleasure and consolation resemble those who followed the Lord, not to hear his teaching, but because they ate of the loaves and were filled.[1] They are ready to say with St. Peter, "Rabbi, it is good for us to be here; and let us put up three shelters."[2] But they do not know what they say. After being intoxicated with the joys of the mountain, they deny the Son of God and refuse to follow him to Calvary. Not only do they desire delights, but they seek illuminations also. The mind is curious to behold, while the heart demands to be filled with soft and flattering emotions. Is this dying to self? Is this the way in which *the just shall live by faith*?[3]

They desire to have unusual revelations that may be regarded as supernatural gifts and a mark of the special favor of God. Nothing is so flattering to self-love. All the greatness of the world at once could not so inflate the heart. These supernatural gifts nourish in secret the life of the old nature. It is an ambition of the most refined character, since it is wholly spiritual. But it is merely ambition, a desire to feel, to enjoy, to possess God and his gifts, to behold his light, to discern spirits, to prophesy—in short, to be an extraordinarily gifted person. For the enjoyment of revelations and delights leads the soul little by little toward a secret coveting of all these things.

Yet the Apostle shows us a *more excellent way*, for which he inspires us to a holy ambition: it is the way of love *which seeks not its own*.[4] It is less in search of pleasure than of God, whose will it longs to fulfill. If this love finds pleasure in devotion, it does not rest in it, but makes it serve to strengthen its weakness, as a convalescent uses a staff to aid him in walking, but throws it aside when he is well again. In the same way the tender and childlike soul whom God fed with milk in the beginning, allows itself to be weaned when he sees that it is time that it should be nourished with strong food.

We must not be always children, always demanding heavenly consolations. We must put away childish things with St. Paul.[5] Our early joys served well to attract us and to draw us away from unrefined and worldly pleasures by others of a purer kind. They led us to a life of prayer and commitment. But to demand to be in a state of constant enjoyment takes away the feeling of the cross, and to live in a fervor of devotion that continually keeps paradise open—this is not dying upon the cross and becoming nothing.

This life of revelations and sensible delights is a very dangerous snare if we become so attached to it as to desire nothing more. Those who have no other attraction to prayer will quit both prayer and God whenever these gratifications disappear. St. Teresa says that a great number of people leave off praying at the very moment when their devotion is beginning to be real. How many there are who, in consequence of too soft an upbringing in Jesus Christ, and too great a fondness for the milk of his word, go back and abandon their interior life as soon as God undertakes to wean them! We need not be astonished at this, for they mistake the portico of the temple for the very sanctuary itself. They desire the death of their unrefined external passion, so that they may lead a delicious life of self-satisfaction within. Hence, so much infidelity and disappointment occurred even among those who appeared the most fervent and most devoted. Those who have talked the loudest of death to self, of the darkness of faith, are often the most surprised and discouraged when they really experience these things and their consolation is taken away.

Souls are earthly in desiring something tangible, as it were, before they can feel firm. But this is all wrong. It is these very things of sense that produce vacillation. We think, while the pleasure lasts, that we shall never desert God. We say in our prosperity that we shall never be moved.[6] But the moment our intoxication is over, we give up all for lost, thus substituting our own pleasure and imagination in place of God. Naked faith alone is a sure guard against illusion. When our foundation is not upon imagination, feeling, pleasure, or extraordinary illumination; when we rest upon God only in unpretentious and plain faith, in the simplicity of the gospel receiving the consolations which he sends, but dwelling in none of them; when we abstain from judging and ever strive to be obedient, believing that it is easy to be deceived and others may be able to set us right—in short, always acting with simplicity and an upright intention, following the light of the faith in each present moment—then we are indeed in a way that is not easily subject to illusion.

Experience will demonstrate better than anything else how much more certain this path is than the path of special revelations, illuminations, and emotional delights. Whoever will try it will soon find that this way of simple faith, strictly followed, is the way to the most complete death of self. Interior delights and revelations secure our self-love against damage—for all its external sacrifices—and lead to the cherishing of a secret and refined life of the old nature. But to allow ourselves to be stripped inwardly and outwardly at once, outwardly by circumstances and inwardly by this dark night of pure faith[7]—this is a total sacrifice and least likely to be subject to self-deception.

Those who seek a constant succession of emotions and certainties are by that very course exposing themselves most surely to deception. On the other hand, those who follow the leadings of the love that strips them and leaves them the faith that walks in darkness, without seeking any other support, avoid all the sources of error and illusion. The author of *My Imitation of Christ* (Book III) tells us that if God takes away our inward delights, it should be our pleasure to remain pleasureless. O how beloved of God is a soul thus crucified who rests calmly upon the cross and desires only to die with Jesus! It is not true to say that on being deprived of feeling we are afraid of having lost God. It is our impatience under the trial, the restlessness of a pampered and dainty nature, a search for some support for self-love, and a secret return to self after our consecration to God. O God, where are they who do not stop in the way? If they persevere to the end, they shall receive a crown of Life!

[1] St. John 6:26.

[2] St. Mark 9:5 (NIV).

[3] Hebrews 10:38.

[4] 1 Corinthians 12:31 and 13:5.

[5] 1 Corinthians 13:11.

[6] Psalm 30:6.

[7] [without being able to *see* what it is all about!]—*Ed.*

thirty-one

The Proper Use of Crosses

It is hard to convince us of the goodness of God in loading those whom he loves with crosses. "Why," we say, "should he take pleasure in causing us to suffer? Could he not make us good without making us miserable?" Yes, doubtless he could, for all things are possible with God. He holds in his omnipotent hands the hearts of men, and turns them as he will, as the skill of the workman can give direction to the stream at the summit of a hill. But able as he may be to save us without crosses, he has not chosen to do it, just as he has not seen fit to create men at once in the full vigor of manhood, but has allowed them to grow up by degrees amid all the dangers and weaknesses of childhood and youth. In this matter, he is the Master; we have only to adore in silence the depths of his wisdom without understanding it.

Nevertheless, we see clearly that we never could become wholly good without becoming humble, unselfish, and disposed to give back everything to God without any restless self-concern.

In detaching us from our self-life and in destroying our self-love, it would take a powerful miracle to keep the work of grace from being painful. Neither in his gracious nor providential dealings does God work a miracle lightly. It would be as great a wonder to see a person full of self become in a moment dead to all self-interest and all sensitiveness, as it would be to see a slumbering infant wake in the morning a fully developed man. God works in mysterious ways in grace as well as in nature, concealing his operations under an unseen succession of events. In this way he keeps us in the darkness of faith. Not only does he accomplish his designs gradually, but he does so by means that appear the most simple and best designed to accomplish the end in view, in order that human wisdom may ascribe the success to the process, and thus make his own working be less evident! Otherwise every act of God would seem to be a miracle, and the state of faith, in which it is God's will that we should live, would come to an end.

This state of faith is necessary, not only to stimulate good souls, causing them to sacrifice their reason in a life full of darkness, but also to blind those who, by their presumption, deserve such a sentence. They behold the works of God, but do not understand them. They can see nothing in them but the results of material laws. They are destitute of true knowledge, for that is only open to those who distrust their own abilities. Proud human wisdom is unworthy to be taken into the counsels of God.

God renders the working of grace slow and obscure, then, so that he may keep us in the darkness of faith. He makes use of the inconstancy and ingratitude of the creature, and he makes use of the disappointments, the surpluses, and the excesses which accompany prosperity, in order to detach us from them both. He frees us from self by revealing our weaknesses and corruptions in a multitude of backslidings. All this dealing appears perfectly natural, and it is by this succession of natural means that we are burnt as by a slow fire. We should like to be consumed at once by the flames of pure love, but such an end would scarcely cost us anything. It is only an excessive self-love that desires to become perfect in a moment and at so cheap a rate.

Why do we rebel against the length of the way? Because we are so wrapped up in self, and God must destroy this infatuation. It is a constant hindrance to his work. Of what can we complain? Our trouble is that we are attached to creatures and still more to self. The operation is painful, but is made necessary by our corruption, and that same corruption makes it distressing. If our flesh were sound, the surgeon would use no knife. He only cuts in proportion to the depth of the wound and the diseased condition of the parts. If we suffer greatly, it is because the evil is great. Is the surgeon cruel because he cuts to the quick? No, on the contrary, it is both love and skill. He would treat his only and well-beloved son.

It is the same way with God. He never afflicts us except against his own inclination. His fatherly heart is not gladdened at the sight of our misery, but he cuts to the quick, that he may heal the disease in our souls. He must snatch away from us whatever we cling to too fondly, and all that we love inordinately, contrary to his claim upon us. He acts in this as we do by our children. They cry because we take away the knife which was their amusement but might have been their death. We weep, we become discouraged, we cry aloud. We are ready to murmur against God, as children get angry with their mothers. But God lets us weep and secures our salvation. He afflicts only to amend. Even when he seems to overwhelm, he means nothing but good: it is only to spare us the evils we were preparing for ourselves. The things we now lament for a little while would have caused us to mourn forever. What we think lost was indeed lost when we seemed to have it, but now God has laid it aside for us that we may inherit it in the eternity so near at hand. He only deprives us of what we cherish to teach us how to love it blamelessly, steadfastly, and moderately, and to secure its eternal enjoyment for us in his own bosom, to do us a thousand times more good than we could ask or think by ourselves. With the exception of sin, nothing happens in this world out of the will of God. He is the Author, Ruler, and Giver of all. He has numbered the hairs of our head, the leaves on the tree, the sand on the seashore, and the drops of the ocean. When he made the universe, his wisdom weighed and measured every atom. He breathes into us the breath of life, and renews it every moment. He knows the numbers of our days, and holds in his all-powerful hand the keys of the tomb to open or to shut.

God is good, tender, compassionate towards our misery, even when he seems to launch his thunders at us, even when we are open-mouthed in our complaints of his severity.

We exaggerate all our sufferings by our cowardice. They are great, it is true, but they are magnified by fear. The way to lessen them is to abandon ourselves courageously into the hands of God. We must suffer, but the aim of our pain is to purify our souls, and make us worthy of him.

thirty-two

Joy in Bearing the Cross

I cannot help admiring the goodness of the cross. We are worth nothing without it. It makes me tremble and convulses me as soon as I begin to feel it. All that I have said of its helpful operations vanishes away before the agony it brings to my inmost heart. But as soon as it gives me time to breathe, I open my eyes again and I see that it is praiseworthy. Then I am ashamed to have been so overwhelmed by it. The experience of this inconsistency is a deep lesson for me.

In whatever state we may be, whatever consequences God may give, we are blessed in being given over to his hands. If we should die, it is in the Lord; if we should live, it is living to him. As St. Teresa has said, "Either to die, or to suffer."

Nothing is more important than the cross, except the perfect reign of God. Indeed, when we suffer with love, his reign has begun in us, and we must be contented with that as long as God defers the consummation.

We need the cross. The faithful Distributor of gifts has allotted our portion to us as well. May he be blessed for ever. Oh, how good he is to chastise us for our correction!

thirty-three

What God Orders Is Best

We may desire to be at liberty, that we may pray to God; and God, who knows so much better than we do what we really want, sends perplexity and restraint so that we become confounded. This trial from the hand of God will be far more help to you than the self-sought sweetness of prayer. You know very well that it is not necessary to be always on retreat in order to love God. When he gives you the time, take it and profit by it. But until then, wait in faith, well persuaded that what he orders is best.

Lift your heart to him frequently by pulling away from the world. Speak only when obliged to, and bear with patience whatever happens to cross you. God treats you according to your necessity, and you have more need of mortification than of illumination!

When you are not permitted to enjoy long seasons of leisure, make the most of the short ones: ten minutes faithfully employed before God in the midst of your distractions will be as valuable to you as whole hours devoted to him in your more unoccupied moments. Moreover, these little odds and ends of time will amount to quite a sum in the course of the day, and will present this advantage, that God will very likely have been more in mind than if you had given it to him all at once. Love, silence, suffering, yielding our own pleasure: such is our portion. We are called to be happy in bearing the burden which God himself lays upon us in the order of his providence.

The crosses that we originate are not nearly as efficient in dealing with self-love as those that come to us in the daily allotments of God. These allotments contribute no food for the nourishment of our own wills, and since they proceed from a merciful providence, they are accompanied by grace sufficient for all our needs. We have nothing to do, then, but to surrender ourselves to God each day, without looking further. He will carry us in his arms as a tender mother bears her child. Let us believe, hope, and love with all the simplicity of little children. In every necessity let us turn a loving and trusting look toward our heavenly Father. For what say the Scriptures? "Can a mother forget the baby at her breast and have no compassion on the child she has borne? Though she may forget, I will not forget you!"[1]

[1] Isaiah 49:15 (NIV).

thirty-four

Keeping All Our Affections in God

When we love anything out of God, says St. Augustine, we love God the less for it. It is like a stream from which part of the water is turned off. This division of the affections of the heart diminishes what should go to God, and it is from such a division that arise all the disturbances of the heart. God wishes to have all, and his jealousy will not leave a divided heart in peace. The least affection outside of him complicates our lives and causes us to feel ill at ease. It is only in an unreserved love for him that the heart deserves to find peace.

The divided heart is the opposite of a recollected one. It awakens all our appetites for created things, dragging the soul and tearing it away from the true Center of its rest. Moreover, it excites the emotions and the imagination, requiring painful labor to quiet them again, and this occupation is an additional kind of inevitable distraction.

Busy yourself as little as possible with all that is external. Give to the concerns that providence lays upon you a quiet and moderate attention at suitable hours. Leave the rest. We do much more by a gentle and tranquil concentration in the presence of God than by the greatest eagerness and all the efforts of our restless nature.

thirty-five

Two Kinds of Love

Why do the gifts of God give more pleasure when they exist in ourselves than when they are given to our neighbor? Why, if we are not attached to self? If we prefer to see them in our own possession rather than in that of those about us, we shall certainly be affected when we see them operating more perfectly in them than they are in us. This constitutes envy. What is to be done? We must rejoice that the will of God is done in us and that his will reigns there not for our happiness and perfection, but for his own good pleasure and glory.

God, in his desire to strip the soul for its own perfection, causes it really to pass through these trials of self, and never lets it alone until he has put an end to its love of self-concern and support. There is nothing so jealous, so exacting, and so searching as this pure love of God. It cannot abide a thousand things that were unnoticed in our previous state. What other Christians might call insignificant seems a vital point to the soul that is intent on the death of the old self. As with gold in the furnace, the fire consumes all that is not gold, so it seems necessary that the heart should be melted with fervent heat, that the love of God may be rendered pure. Those being thus purified are thankful to God for whatever he does in them solely because he does it for his own glory.

God does not pursue every soul in this way in the present life. There are many truly good persons whom he leaves in some degree under the sway of self-love. These remainders of self help support them in the practice of virtue and serve to purify them to a certain degree. There would be almost nothing more harmful or dangerous than to deprive such persons of the contemplation of the grace of God in them as leading to their own personal perfection. This second group are also grateful, but partly because their *own* perfection is secured at the same time. If the first group should try to deprive the second of this interior comfort they have in reference to grace, they would cause them as much injury as they would an infant by weaning it before it was able to eat. To take away the breast would be to destroy it. We must never seek to deprive a soul of the food which still contains nutriment for it, and which God allows to remain as a stay to its weakness. To forestall or hinder grace would be to destroy it.

On the other hand, the second group should not condemn the first because they do not see them as much concerned as they are themselves about their own perfection. God works in every one as he pleases. The wind blows where it pleases,[1] and *as* it pleases. Forgetfulness of self is a state in which God can do with us whatever most pleases him. The important point is, those who are still supported somewhat by self should not be too anxious about those who are in pure love, nor should the latter try to make the former pass through new trials before God calls them to it.

[1] See St. John 3:8.

thirty-six

Our Union in God

Let us all remain in our only Center, where we can always find each other, and where we are all but one and the same. Oh, how miserable it is to be separate from one another! We must be only one! I wish to know nothing but that unity. All that goes beyond that comes from division and self-seeking.

Friends are separated and consequently they scarcely love each other at all, or love each other very badly. The "I" loves itself too much to be able to love that which is called "him" or "her." And those who have but one single love have stripped off the "I," and love nothing but in God and for God alone.

Those who are engrossed in self-love, love their neighbor only in themselves and for themselves. Let us then be united by being nothing except in our common Center, where all is blended together without a shadow of distinction. It is there that I will meet you, and we will dwell together. It is at this indivisible point that China and Canada join hands. It is here that all distances are annihilated.

In the name of God, be simple, humble, open, unreserved, and distrustful of self. God will give you all you need through others, without giving it to you for yourself. Believe humbly, live by faith alone, and it shall be given to you in proportion as you have believed.

thirty-seven

Bearing Suffering

Kiss lovingly the Hand that strikes you. Formerly you abused your health, and the pleasures which health gives. The weakness and the pain which now have taken the place of health are your natural penance. May God humble your mind even more than your body, and while he comforts your body according to its needs, may he entirely free you from your deceptions about yourself.

We are truly strong when we cease to believe in our strength, when we feel nothing but the weakness and the limited powers of our own spirit! Then we become ready to think we may be mistaken, and to confess that it is so by correcting ourselves. Then our minds are open to the opinions of others, and we despise nothing but ourselves and our own ideas. We decide nothing, and we say the most positive things in the simplest tone and in a manner that is most considerate of others. We willingly allow others to judge us, we yield without difficulty, and we give the first comer the right to rebuke or correct us. At the same time we never judge anyone except from a real necessity. We only speak to persons who wish us to speak to them, and while we are telling them of the imperfections we see in them, we do so without laying down the law, as if we would prefer to be silent rather than speaking as if we took pleasure in our criticism.

This is the health I desire for you in your mind, with a real cure in your body. And while you are waiting for this, bear your suffering with humility and patience.

thirty-eight

Suffering Rightly

We know that we must suffer, and that we deserve it. Nevertheless, we are always surprised at affliction, as if we thought we neither merited nor had need of it.

Only true and pure love delights to endure, for nothing else is perfectly abandoned. Resignation induces us to bear pain, but there is something in it that is afflicted in suffering and resists. The resignation that measures out its abandonment to God with selfish reflection is willing to suffer, but is constantly examining to make sure whether it suffers acceptably. In fact, the resigned soul is composed as it were of two persons: one keeping the other in subjection, and watching, lest it should revolt.

In love that is unselfish and abandoned, the soul is fed in silence on the cross and in its union with the crucified Savior, without any reflections on the severity of its sufferings. There exists but a single, simple will, which permits God to see it just as it is, without trying to behold itself. It says nothing, does nothing. What, then, does it do? It suffers. And is this all? Yes, all. It has nothing else to do but suffer. Love can be heard easily enough without speech or thought. It does all that it is required to do, which is to have no will when it is stripped of all consolation. The purest of all loves is a will so filled with the will of God that there remains nothing else.

What a consolation it is that we are then rid of so many anxieties about our exercise of patience and the other virtues in the sight of those about us! It is enough to be humbled and abandoned in the midst of suffering. This is not courage; it is something both more and less: less in the eyes of the ordinary class of Christians; more in the eyes of pure faith. It is a humiliation that raises the soul into all the greatness of God. It is a weakness that strips us of every resource in order to bestow upon us his omnipotence. "When I am weak," says St. Paul, "then I am strong. I can do everything through him who gives me strength."[1]

When undergoing suffering it is enough to feed on some short sentences suited to our condition and our taste, with frequent interruptions to quiet the senses and make room for the inward spirit of recollection. We sometimes suffer, scarcely knowing that we are in distress; at other times we suffer, and know that we are not bearing it well, but we carry this second and heavier cross without impatience. True love goes ever straightforward, not in its own strength, but counting itself as nothing. Then indeed we are truly happy. The cross is no longer a cross when there is no *self* to suffer under it and to appropriate its good and evil.

[1] 2 Corinthians 12:10; Philippians 4:13 (NIV).

thirty-nine

The Usefulness of Deprivations

Follow faithfully the light that God gives you to die to the refinements and sensibilities of your self-love. When we give ourselves entirely to the designs of God for us, we are as willing to be deprived of consolations as to enjoy them. Often a deprivation that disturbs and humbles us is more useful to us than an abundance of comforting.

Why should it not be useful for us to be deprived of the presence and advice of a friend, when it is sometimes very wholesome for us to be deprived of the sense of the presence and of the consoling gifts of God himself? God is very near us when he *seems* far away from us, *if* we bear this apparent absence of his in a spirit of love for him and of death to ourselves.

Accustom yourself gradually to this burden. When children

begin to grow, they make a change from the milk of a tender mother who carries them in her bosom, to walking alone and eating dry bread.

forty

The Value of Moderation

Be careful never to become really lax. Avoid dissipation and all social contacts and friendships that might bring back your taste for the world, and that might diminish the grace that is within you.

Do not visit with others too much. Do not fatigue yourself, either with too much study or with unhealthy solitude—not even with your exercise of devotion. Take everything with moderation. Change and diversify your occupations, and do not become too engrossed in any of them too eagerly. Stop as soon as you feel a certain eagerness that arises from passion. Mistrust your own determined and superior spirit. As soon as a word of haughty disdain escapes from your lips, take a lower tone immediately. Never judge others except from necessity. Never allow yourself any little deception with the view of making yourself appear better to others than you really are. God will be with you if you have in your heart an upright and simple intention of carrying out all this.

You *will* fail, but you must not be discouraged. And while you humble yourself for your faults, you must go on your way again, and repair the false steps where self-love has caused you to stumble.

forty-one

Regarding Prayer

In regard to prayer, always propose to yourself some simple and solid subject that is of practical use in attaining the virtues of the gospel. If you find no food for your soul in a given subject, and if you feel an attraction and ability to simply remain in the presence of God, remain so as long as you are so drawn. But never make it a rule for yourself, and always be faithful in proposing a special subject of thought and meditation to yourself, to see if it can occupy and nourish you. Receive without resistance the insights and feelings which may come to you in prayer, but do not trust any of these things which might flatter your pride and fill you with vain self-complacency.

It is better to be very humble and very much ashamed after the faults we have committed than to be pleased with our prayer and think that we are very much advanced after having had many fine feelings and grand thoughts while we were praying to God. Let all such things pass. They may be helps sent to us from God, but we must remember that they may be turned into very dangerous delusions if we dwell upon them ever so little to seek our own pleasure in them.

The great point is to mortify our *selves*, to obey the Lord, to distrust ourselves, and to carry our cross.

forty-two

Keeping a Spirit of Prayer

Never be discouraged about your faults. Bear with your-self while you are trying to correct them, as you would bear with and correct your neighbor. Give up a certain activity of mind that wears out your body and makes you commit many faults. Accustom yourself gradually to extend your prayer over all the outward activities of the day. Speak, act, and work in peace as if you were in prayer, for indeed you should be so.

Do everything without overeagerness, by the spirit of grace. As soon as you perceive that your natural activity is slipping in, enter again quietly within yourself where God reigns. Listen to that which the leading of grace demands of you, and then say and do only what that leading inspires. You will be more tranquil for this, and your words will be fewer and more effective for it. While you labor less, you will do many more useful things. It is not a question of a perpetual struggle of the head. That would be impracticable. It is a question of accustoming yourself to a certain peace in which you can easily consult the Beloved of your soul as to what you ought to do. This consultation, very simple and very brief, will be made much more easily with him than the hurried and tumultuous deliberation which we generally have with ourselves when we give way to our natural impetuosity.

When the heart has already a tendency toward God, we can easily accustom ourselves to suspend the hasty movements of nature, and wait for the second moment when we can act through grace by listening to God. It is the continual death of self that constitutes the life of faith. This death is a sweet life, because grace gives peace. It takes the place of nature, nature which only brings us trouble.

Try to accustom yourself to this dependence upon the inner spirit, and then by degrees everything will become prayer. You will still suffer, but a peaceful suffering is only half a suffering.

forty-three

When Spiritual Emotions Fade

It is good to feel how weak we are, and to learn by experience that emotional fervor comes and goes. When we have it, it is God who gives it out of his condescension, to sustain our weakness. It is the milk given to little children. Afterwards we must be weaned and eat the dry bread of persons of mature age.

If we were always to have this delight and skill in devotion without any interruption, we should be strongly tempted to look upon it as our permanent possession. We should no longer feel our weakness or our inclination to sin. We should not have sufficient distrust of ourselves, and we should not come to prayer with sufficient humility.

But when this emotional fervor declines or disappears, we feel that we have lost something. We recognize where it came from, and we are forced to humble ourselves, so that we may find it again in God. The less satisfaction we feel in serving him, the more fidelity we exercise in it. We restrain ourselves, we sacrifice our inclinations. We no longer proceed by the help of winds and sails, but by rowing hard against the current. We take all upon ourselves. We are in darkness, and we have to content ourselves with faith alone. We are in sorrow and bitterness, but we are willing to be so, and it is no longer through pleasure that we hold fast to God. We are ready to receive that pleasure again as soon as God restores it. We recognize our own weakness, and we understand that when God *does* restore the enjoyment to us, it is in pity for our weakness. But when he deprives us of it, we bear the deprivation in peace, and we are sure that God knows much better than we do what is necessary for us.

That which depends on us, and which ought always to be uniform, is our good will. This will is even the more pure when it is quite dry and quite bare without ever being lax.

Be as firm in observing your hours of prayer as if you still had the greatest pleasure and ease in them. Profit even by any time in the day when you are only half-occupied in outward activities. It is only in conversation that the practice of this presence is more difficult. Nevertheless, we can often renew within ourselves that general thought of God which can regulate all our words and repress our all-too-lively flashes of wit when we are conversing with others—all our touches of pride or superiority—all the refinements of our self-love.

Bear with yourself, but do not flatter yourself. Labor effectively and constantly to correct your faults, but do so peacefully, and without the impatience that comes of self-love.

forty-four

Dealing with Sickness and Grief

You know that illness is a precious gift that God gives us to make us feel the weakness of our soul by the weakness of our body. We flatter ourselves that we despise this life and long for the heavenly country, but when age or sickness make us see our end much nearer, self-love awakens, pities itself, and is alarmed. We do not find in the depths of our heart any desire for the kingdom of God. We find only sloth, cowardice, lukewarmness, disunity, and attachment to all those things from which we thought we had been freed. Such a humiliating experience is often more useful for us than all the emotional feelings upon which perhaps we were relying a little too much. The great point is to give ourselves up to the Spirit of grace, and allow ourselves to be detached from everything here below.

Receive with childlike simplicity all the comforts which you are given. Thinking upon God, peace, obedience, the sacrifice of your life, patience in your infirmities—these will be sufficiently great mortifications.

When we have lost someone dear to us and God takes away a great source of comfort, it is because he wishes to deprive us of it through the jealousy of his love. He finds, even in the most lawful and the purest friendships, certain secret movements of self-love. These he wishes to cut down at their deepest roots. Let him do what he will. Adore this severity which is only love. Enter into his designs. Why should we weep for those who weep no more, and whose tears God has forever wiped away? It is for ourselves that we weep, and we must allow our humanity to be thus touched with its own grief. But faith assures us that we shall soon be reunited with those whom our senses indicate as lost to us.

Live by faith without paying attention to flesh and blood. You will find again the friend who has departed from your eyes, in our common Center, which is the Bosom of God. Calm your spirit before God. Do not fear to comfort your imagination by the help of some gentle and pious social contacts. We must not be ashamed to treat ourselves like children when we feel the need of such treatment.

forty-five

Bearing Spiritual Dryness

Do you no longer find the same peace of mind in your devotions which was so easy and so usual with you earlier? God is accustoming you to a fidelity that is less sweet and more painful to nature. If such ease in concentrating yourself on God were always equal, it would give you a support that would be too tied to feelings, and, as it were, too natural. In such a case you would experience no interior cross and no weakness. It is necessary for you to feel your misery. The humiliation that follows will be more useful to you than the most consoling spiritual fervor if you bear it patiently without being discouraged.

We must never give up prayer. We must bear the loss of that which it pleases God to take away from us, but we may not take anything away from ourselves, nor are we allowed to let anything be lost through voluntary negligence.

Continue to pray, but make your prayer in the simplest and freest manner, so that you may not fret over it. Make use of all that can renew the sense of the presence of God without any uneasy effort. During the course of the day, avoid everything that might distract you or attract you, or excite your natural vivacity. Calm yourself as much as you can on every occasion, and pass by all that is not the concern of the present moment. "Each day has enough trouble of its own."[1] Bear your dryness and your involuntary distractions as your principal cross.

It may be helpful in such spiritual dryness to try a little retreat, but we must not carry it too far. We may comfort our imagination according to our needs by such things as are compatible with the presence of God.

[1] St. Matthew 6:34 (NIV).

forty-six

Using Time Wisely

It is essential to employ all our time to good purposes. Grace has long since convinced you of this. It is a pleasant thing to come into contact with those who understand this, but there is a tremendous distance between the conviction of the intellect, even combined with the good intention of the heart, and a faithful and exact obedience.

Nothing has been more common in ancient as well as in modern times than to meet souls who were perfect and holy, *theoretically!* "You shall know them by their fruits," says the Savior.[1] This is the only rule that never deceives, when it is properly understood. It is that by which we must judge ourselves.

There is a time for everything in our lives, but the maxim that governs every moment is that there should be none useless; that every moment shall enter into the order and progress of our salvation; that they are all accompanied by duties which God has allotted with his own hand, and of which he will demand an account. For from the first instant of our existence to the last, he has never designed for us a barren moment, nor one which we can consider as given up to our own discretion. The great thing is to recognize his will in relation to them. This is not to be effected by an eager and restless seeking, which is much more likely to spoil everything than to enlighten us as to our duty. It is accomplished by a true submission to those whom God has set over us and by a clean and upright heart which seeks God in its simplicity and vigorously opposes all the deceit and false wisdom of self as fast as it is revealed. We misuse our time, not only when we do wrong or do nothing, but also when we do something else than what we *should* have done at that moment, even though it may be the means of good. We are strangely ingenious in perpetually seeking our own interest, and what the world does nakedly and without shame, those who desire to be devoted to God do in a refined manner under the cover of some pretext which serves as a veil to hide the deformity of their conduct from them.

In general, the best means to ensure the profitable use of our time is to accustom ourselves to living in continual dependence upon the Spirit of God and his law; to receive what he is pleased to bestow at every instant; to consult him in every emergency that requires instant action; to flee to him in our weaker moments, when strength seems to fail, invoking his aid; and to raise our hearts to him whenever we are enticed by material things, and find ourselves estranged from God and far from the true road.

Happy is the soul that commits itself into the hands of its Creator, ready to do all his will, and continually cries, "Lord, what wilt thou have me to do? Teach me to do your will, for you are my God!"[2]

During our necessary occupations, we need to pay only an effortless attention to the leadings of divine providence. As they are all prepared for us and presented by him, our only care should be to receive them with a childlike spirit, submitting everything absolutely to him: temper, will, scruples, restlessness, self-reflections, overflowing emotions of hurry, vain joy, or anything else in the different events of the day that pleases or displeases us. Let us be careful, however, not to allow ourselves to be overwhelmed by the multiplicity of our exterior occupations, no matter what they may be.

Let us endeavor to begin every enterprise with the sole aim to commit it to the glory of God, continue it with composure, and finish it with patience.

Intervals of relaxation and amusement are the most dangerous seasons for us, and perhaps the most useful for others. We must be on our guard that we be as faithful as possible to the presence of God. We must make use of all that Christian vigilance so much recommended by our Lord. We can raise our hearts to God in a simple act of faith and dwell in sweet and peaceful dependence upon the Spirit of grace as the only means of our safety and strength. This is especially necessary for those who are looked up to as an authority, and whose words may be the cause of so much good or evil. Our leisure hours are ordinarily the sweetest and pleasantest for ourselves. No employment of them is better than refreshing our spiritual strength by secret and intimate communion with God. Prayer is so necessary and the source of so many blessings, that they who have discovered the treasure cannot be prevented from having recourse to it whenever they have an opportunity.

[1] St. Matthew 7:16 (KJV, SLIGHTLY MODIFIED).
[2] Psalm 143:10 (NIV).

forty-seven

Preserving Peace
with Others

To be really pleased even with the best persons, we must be satisfied with little and we must bear with much. The most perfect people have many imperfections. We also have imperfections, and great ones. Our faults, joined to theirs, make our bearing with each other very difficult. But bear one another's burdens, and so you shall fulfill the law of Christ.[1] We must make a charitable allowance in this matter. Frequent silence, habitual recollection, prayer, detachment from ourselves, renunciation of all the carefully crafted criticisms, faithfulness in abandoning all vain judgments of a jealous and fastidious self-love—all these things tend very much to preserve peace and union with God. We spare ourselves much trouble by this simplicity. Happy are those who pay no attention to self-love, and who pay no attention to the criticism of others.

Content yourself with leading a simple life according to your circumstances. For the rest, obey the Lord and bear your little daily crosses. You need them, and God gives them to you only out of pure mercy. The great thing is to make light of yourself sincerely, and to consent to be made light of by others if God permits it. Nourish yourself with him alone. St. Augustine says that his mother lived only by prayer. We also are to live by prayer and die to all the rest. We can live to God only by a continual death to self.

[1] Cf. Galatians 6:2.

forty-eight

True Liberty

When we are no longer embarrassed by the restless reflections of self, we begin to enjoy true liberty.

False wisdom, on the other hand—always on the watch, ever occupied with self, constantly jealous of its own perfection—suffers severely whenever it is permitted to perceive the smallest speck of imperfection. Those who are single-minded and detached from self labor toward the attainment of perfection, and are more successful in proportion as they forget themselves and never dream of virtue in any other light than as something that accomplishes the will of God.

The source of all our defects is the love of self. Everything is pointed to that instead of to the love of God. Whoever, then, labors to get rid of self, to deny him-*self* according to the instructions of Christ, strikes at once at the root of every evil, and finds, in this simple abandonment of self, the germ of every good.

Then those words of Scripture are heard within and understood, "Where the Spirit of the Lord is, there is freedom."[1] We neglect nothing that will cause the kingdom of God to come both within and without, but in the midst of our frailties we are at peace. We would rather die than commit the slightest voluntary sin, but we have no fear for our reputation from the judgment of man. We welcome sharing the reproach of Christ Jesus and dwell in peace though surrounded by uncertainties. The judgments of God do not frighten us, for we have abandoned ourselves to them, imploring his mercy according to our attainments in confidence, sacrifice, and absolute surrender. The greater the abandonment, the more flowing the peace. It sets us in such a spacious place that we are prepared for everything. We will *everything* and we will *nothing*. We are as guileless as babes.

Our illumination from God uncovers the lightest transgressions, but never discourages us. We walk before him, but if we stumble, we hasten to resume our way, and have no watchword but *Onward!*

If we would find God, we must destroy the remains of the old Adam within. The Lord held a little child in his arms when he declared, "The kingdom of heaven belongs to such as these."[2] The sum of the principal directions for attaining true liberty without neglecting our duties is this: do not reason too much; always have an upright purpose in the smallest matters; and pay no attention to the thousand reflections by which we wrap and busy ourselves in self under the pretense of correcting our faults.

[1] 2 Corinthians 3:17 (NIV).
[2] St. Matthew 19:14 (NIV).

forty-nine

Dealing with a Haughty Spirit

A proud or disdainful manner, one that relishes ridicule or censoriousness, indicates a self-satisfied mind that is unconscious of its own weak points. It is a prey to its hard-to-please tastes and finds pleasure in the troubles of others. There is nothing more humbling than this sort of pride, so easily wounded, disdainful, contemptuous, haughty, jealous of its own rights, undisposed to forgive others. It is a proof that one is very imperfect indeed when one is so impatient with the imperfections of others. There is no remedy for all this save hoping in God, who is as good and powerful as you are weak and bad. Yet probably he will let you grovel on at length without uprooting your natural disposition and long-formed habits. That is because it is far better for you to be crushed by your own frailty and by the proof of your incapacity to escape from it, than to enjoy a sudden advance toward perfection.

Only strive to bear with others and turn your eyes away from people who cannot edify you, as you would turn them from temptation. They really are a very dangerous temptation to you. Pray, read, humble yourself by cultivating lowly things. Soften your heart by uniting it to Jesus in his patience and humiliation. Seek strength in silence.

fifty

Thinking of Death

There comes an age when the thought of death puts itself forward and forces itself upon our consideration much more often and much more strongly than before. Moreover, there comes a time of retirement in which we have fewer distractions with regard to this great subject. God even makes use of this severe trial to take away our self-deceptions about our courage, to make us feel our weakness, and to keep us very humble in his hands.

Nothing is more humiliating than a troubled imagination in which we can no longer find our former trust in God. It is the crucible of humiliation in which our heart is purified by the conviction of its weakness and unworthiness. The Holy Spirit says, "No one living is righteous before you."[1] It is also written that the heavens are not pure in the sight of our

Judge.[2] It is certain that "we stumble in many ways."[3] We see our faults and we do not see our virtues. It would be very dangerous for us to see them even if they were real!

What we have to do is walk uprightly and without laxness in the midst of this trouble, just as we tried to walk in the ways of God before trouble came upon us. If this trouble shows us something in ourselves that needs correction, we must be faithful to this light in the first place, but we must do so under the guidance of a good counselor, so that we may not fall into legalistic scruples. Afterward, when we have seen our faults, we must remain in peace and pay no attention to the self-love that tries to make us pity ourselves at the thought of our own death. We must detach ourselves from this life, make a sacrifice of it to God, and abandon ourselves to him with confidence.

When St. Ambrose was dying, they asked if he was not troubled with fear of the judgments of God. He replied, "We have a good Master." This is the answer which we must give to ourselves. It is necessary for us to die in an impenetrable uncertainty, not only about the judgments of God upon us, but about our own dispositions. As St. Augustine says, we must be reduced so low that we can offer to God only "our misery and his mercy." Our misery is the proper object of his mercy, and his mercy is our only claim. While you are in this state of sadness, read all that can encourage your confidence and console your heart. "Surely God is good to Israel, to those who are pure in heart!"[4] Ask of him that uprightness of heart that pleases him so much and makes him so compassionate to our weakness.

---

[1] Psalm 143:2 (NIV, SLIGHTLY MODIFIED).

[2] Job 15:15.

[3] James 3:2 (NIV, SLIGHTLY MODIFIED).

[4] Psalm 73:1 (NIV).

fifty-one

The Cross as a Treasure

We must carry the cross as a treasure. It is through the cross that we are made worthy of God and conformed to the likeness of his Son. Crosses are a part of our daily bread. God regulates the measure of them according to our real wants, which he knows, and of which we are ignorant. Let him do as he wills, and let us resign ourselves into his hands.

Be a child of divine providence. Leave it to your relatives and friends to reason about things. Do not think about the future from afar. The manna was corrupted when, out of prudent foresight, they wished to provide sufficient supply for more than one day. Do not say, What shall we do tomorrow? "Tomorrow will worry about itself."[1] Confine yourself today to your present needs. God will give you each day the help that is proportioned to that day. "Those who seek the

Lord lack no good thing."[2] Providence would do miracles for us, but we hinder these miracles by trying to anticipate them. We make for ourselves, by our restless industry, a providence as defective as the providence of God would be certain.

Be faithful and docile. By an infinite distrust of yourself make your weaknesses profitable, and by a childlike pliability allow yourself to be corrected. Humility will be your strength, even in the midst of weakness.

I do not doubt that our Lord will always treat you as one of his friends; that is to say, he will send you crosses, sufferings, and humiliations. These ways and means, which God makes use of to draw souls to himself, do this work so much better and more quickly than the creature's own efforts; for the very fact of its being God's action alone is destructive to self-love and tears up the roots which we cannot even discover without great difficulty. But God, who knows all the secret lurking places of self-love, proceeds forthwith to attack it in its stronghold, and upon its own ground.

If we were strong enough and faithful enough to trust ourselves entirely to God, and to follow him simply wherever he wished to lead us, we should have no need of great application of mind to labour in the work of our perfection. But because we are so weak in faith that we wish to know where we are going, without trusting to God, our way becomes much longer, and spoils our spiritual affairs.

Abandon yourself as much as you can to God, until your last breath, and he will never forsake you.

[1] St. Matthew 6:34 (NIV).
[2] Psalm 34 :10 (NIV).